You Are Special

Other Books by Tom Sullivan:
If You Could See What I Hear
(with Derek Gill)
Adventures in Darkness

You Are Special

by Tom Sullivan

ideals
PUBLISHING CORPORATION
11315 WATERTOWN PLANK RD.
MILWAUKEE, WISCONSIN 53226

ISBN 0-89542-079-1 395

Published by Ideals Publishing Corporation
11315 Watertown Plank Road
Milwaukee, WI 53226
Published simultaneously in Canada

Photographs by Steve Schatzberg

To my mother, the first person who realized that I was special and spent her life fulfilling my special dreams.

Contents

Preface

When I was a little boy, I used to hear my mother say, "Remember, you are special." I found myself not sure what she meant and not thinking much about it at all. That attitude seems to permeate our society; most of us don't think very much about our own uniqueness.

It is my hope in writing this book to revamp your assertion of yourself, not with gimmicks or formulas for immediate success, but with examples and comments that will stimulate you to find your own direction. If you can read these pages and come to experience an absolute commitment to your own specialness, a belief that that specialness is defined within who you are, that it represents the celebration

Tom and his guide dog, Dinah,
enjoying a moment of fun on the rocks.

of your own uniqueness and the establishment of your own self-image, then the book has performed its correct function. If, on the other hand, you read it and find that the examples noted are "fine for other people" but don't fit you, or that I have not given informative insights that benefit you, then I am very, very sorry.

I believe in the premise of this work, and I have had good reason to feel sorry for myself and feel that other people's input could not be of extensive benefit to me. Being blind made me feel that no one else could understand the world in which I lived; but time has proven that attitude wrong. It is true that other people who are not sightless cannot fully understand what it is to live within the world of a blind person; but the decisions all of us have to make, those personal decisions to establish ourselves as important human beings, never ever change. Only the situation that governs our approach changes; those moments of truth fluctuate based on our own human nuances.

So read this book, willing to accept the truth about yourself, willing to wrestle with the problem of whether or not you are facing life with the best of what you are as a human being, appreciating your own uniqueness, celebrating it, and reveling in the development of your own specialness. There is absolutely no question about whether you can become all the things you want to be. I have experienced and witnessed far too many examples of human beings under stress who have asserted the best that they are, and I will not accept less than that from anyone.

My hope is that you will read these pages and assert those qualities that make you the best that you can be. No one can come to this essence of who *you* are and what *you* are going to do about it except *you*, but I totally believe in your ability to grow. I believe in the human spirit, and I believe that this book can make a small contribution to your evolvement. The pages are written with all the love and excitement that I feel about life. Please feel that excitement with me.

Common Senses

"Eye hath not seen, nor ear heard, . . . the things which God hath prepared for them that love him." What Paul wrote represents a promise of eternal happiness; but present happiness and, indeed, who we are, are shaped right here on earth. We search for our own specialness through confrontation with others and our surroundings, and we understand ourselves through our "common" senses. What wonders of creation! These antennae that reach out to bring us such complex, but joyous, data. I believe that, because of the immediacy of visual stimulation, most of us have not taken the time to examine the sensory possibilities that make up our existence. Come, take a sensory adventure with me and we'll

Tom and Dinah leaving home for their
morning run.

discover how little we know.

A Sensory Adventure

Most people begin their day with the abrupt sound of a buzzing or ringing alarm clock. If they are into pop music, they might awaken to the turned-on sounds of a hyperactive disc jockey (who probably doesn't feel any better than they do but is getting paid to pretend he does) announcing that the day is beautiful and everybody should have been up hours ago.

Touch

My first sensory input, however, is much more personal and is based on touch rather than sound. The touch may not be romantic but is certainly loving. I tend to sleep on my back; and precisely at 6:30, two paws come to rest on my chest and the warm, wet lick of my golden retriever signals that I'd better crawl out of bed and begin my day. I don't get up easily, and Dinah has to apply her morning love three or four times before I put one foot in front of the other and head toward the bathroom, where I find my running shoes and fumble for a clean T-shirt. After somehow getting my fingers to work enough to lace my shoes, I take Dinah out to the backyard, give her a few moments of personal peace and quiet, and then begin my sensory assessment of the day.

Sound

My yard is heavily shaded by high, wide-branched trees, so my first awareness is of the sound of the wind whistling through the leaves. It tells me what kind of run I am in for. If it's windy, I know that when I turn back for home, running southwest, I'm going to be in for a struggle along the ocean.

Smell

On this particular morning, the California coastline is laden with a thick fog bank that doesn't roll away until noontime and has its own special smell. The fog keeps new vapors from rising into the atmosphere, and the air is filled with a potpourri of sensual and sensory stimuli creating, for even the dullest antennae, an excitement that just cannot be tuned out.

The wind reaches out to bring me orange blossoms with their nose-tickling sweetness combined with the pervasive sea air, a freshly fertilized yard, summer roses, morning bacon, fresh-brewed coffee, and newly cut grass. All of these odors are dominated, however, by the acrid, sinus-clearing smell of the beautiful eucalyptus trees indigenous to the area of southern California in which we live.

What an astounding mechanism the brain is to be able on an early morning, when I am still half asleep, to assimilate and distinguish these many incredible creations of Mother Nature's chemistry lab. And this is only the beginning of my morning sensory adventure. Soon I begin to be anxious to hear my feet running on the hard, wet sand of a California beach. Figuring that Dinah has had enough time to herself, I call her into the house and strap on the hard leather harness that connects guide dog and man in a personal world of interdependence and joy.

With a Little Help

There is a wonderful feeling of oneness when I grab that handle and hear Dinah's paws click their way along the cement road in front of my house, taking both of us through my suburban neighborhood to the beach. Although Dinah is doing most of the work, my sensory antennae are operating fully, with sound and smell leading the way, gathering important information about the direction we are going and possible obstacles. Somebody's sprinklers are spitting back and forth across his front lawn; and although Dinah is pointing it out, I have already realized I have to move to the right to avoid getting wet. It's Thursday, and I can smell garbage cans that are waiting for collection, making me aware that Dinah must make some very complicated moves to ensure that I don't upset one. There is a lot of loose dirt under my feet, warning me that I'd better take care; there might be some new construction going on that I don't know about. This last piece of information means that touch has kicked in; and I know that taste won't be far behind because, as we come around the bend leading toward the beach, I take a big breath of air and *taste* the ocean. What a marvelous sensation, maybe even superior to a good wine—it is certainly more alive.

At this point, it's as if the senses are competing for priority in my awareness center. Sound has just jumped back in front again. Have you ever stood high on a bridge and listened to the traffic move back and forth beneath you? Well, that's something like what I hear as I get to the top of the cliff, for down below, the ocean ebbs its way into my sensory experience. It is the most humbling moment I face as a human being on this planet. Here is the power of unlimited tons of water, coming and going, washing and rolling, carrying with it untold mysteries of little-known life forms, each one struggling for its own existence. I'm so ultimately alive, knowing that for the next hour I'm going to commune with both my own body and all the natural wonders in a senso-round of boundless experience.

A Morning Run

I've now arrived on the beach and slipped off my running shoes to touch the dry, soft top-sand, then sink into the wet, high-tidal sand beneath. Dinah and I make our way down the slope of the beach toward the edge of the ocean where the low tide has caused a wide, flat, hard surface, helping aching legs to relax and allowing the body to run free and easily. A gust of cool wind sends a shiver down my back, telling me that my reverie is over for the moment and I'd better get started. The sun hasn't come up yet, so there is still a morning chill in the air. I begin running lazily, not quite committed. My feet hit the sand from toe to heel, toe to heel, shuffling along without any defined rhythm. It stays this way for about a mile-and-a-half. I know it's a mile-and-a-half because just above the cliff is a restaurant. I have never eaten there and never want to. Not because the food is bad, but because the smell of all those breakfasts cooking, mixed with the ocean air and carried by the wind which is already filled with sensations, has to be better than what I'm sure is great cuisine.

A Change Is Noted

The angle of the beach has just changed. My right foot is now higher than my left, and the sand has become grainy. That means that I am at the two-mile point and it is time to start running a little harder. The waves have changed, too. From an easy, constant ebb and flow, they now rush in and rip out the rocky pebbles on their return. Even on a day when the surf is light, one wave probably drives as much dirt as a bulldozer could in a month. The difference is that the next wave returns it.

I'm reaching the two-and-a-half mile point now.

I can tell because there is a pier that juts out in the bay. Sea gulls turn and even an occasional pelican circles high above, waiting for the fishing boats to drop some of the waste from their catch; then those incredible birds dive into the ocean to pick up their morning meal. Their shrieking and the smell of fish let me know that it is time to turn around.

I'm feeling good now. The sound of my own breath as I take in great gulps of ocean air is even with the rhythm of my feet digging footprints along untracked sand. Now the wind is in my face and the salt spray cools me with a blast of needed refreshment. Do you know that salt dried on your skin has a terrific smell? Some people like to shower right after they swim to get rid of the salt water. But I like to let it dry and smell its freshness.

Anyway, the waves have changed again. Whipped by the wind, they foam in diagonals over my feet, swirling sand, salt, and spray at crazy angles to what I hope is the straight line that Dinah and I are running. When this happens, I know that I've come around the last curve and that we have one mile of straight, hard sand to run.

My body is beginning to hurt now, but it's a wonderful hurt. It's the best kind of hurt because I believe I can beat it. I can run even faster. My stride is extending; the footprints are getting wider and wider apart.

The tide has come in just a little, and my feet

splash through ringlets of ocean, making a new and exciting sound. I can smell seaweed and hear the waves changing again. This time they are roaring upon large jetty rocks and I know that there are two hundred yards to go.

"Now, run, Tom, get something out of it . . . feet pounding now . . . faster now . . . Dinah galloping flat out. . . . " It's 7:45. The kids' buses are arriving at the junior high school up the hill. My time was good today. I can hear the diesel engine and know that I have one hundred and fifty yards to run. "Flat out effort now . . . deep breath . . . try to stay with it . . . be alive."

Rewards

All at once it's over and I fill my nostrils and lungs with that terrific sea air, taking in huge gulps to revitalize, oxidize, and help bring down my pounding pulse and heart. Now pull off that shirt and make a final dash toward the cold Pacific Ocean.

"The waves rush toward me . . . sound comes closer . . . Dinah runs free now . . . water touches my ankles, reaches my calves, touches my knees . . . a wave buffets us both . . . knocks me off balance . . . but we've achieved deep enough water to plunge under it and close out sound. My body tingles with the cold sensation . . . head breaks the surface . . . strokes working . . . Dinah is breathing as she swims beside me . . . we break through the surf and find quiet . . .

two hundred yards from shore I roll on my back . . . the waves seem at great distance even though I know we are close to shore . . . the only sound that is vivid is Dinah's rhythmic breathing as she treads water next to me."

I believe I am on top of the world because I have achieved a wondrous communing with nature—a participation that I am lucky enough to have the right to. And, each time, I am aware that I have enjoyed my morning on four magnificent levels of sensory phenomena. At that moment, more than any other, I have no regrets about not being able to see. At that moment, floating easily, being tossed up and down on the blue Pacific, I don't care what color it is. I don't care that I will never see its color, because I know I have come to understand its nuances. It holds for me a special participation . . . a unique involvement of other gifts.

We must finally make our way back to shore and dry off before we head home for Patty's well-deserved breakfast—dog food with maybe a little touch of hamburger for Dinah; hot, fresh coffee, bacon, and fried eggs for me; and, maybe if I'm not too salty, a hug or two from Patty. As we come out of the water, we are both hit by the cold. Dinah quickly finds the shared pile of leash, harness, towel, shirt, and shoes; and drying ourselves as fast as we can, we start up the hill toward home.

Ah, but the sensory gods are not done with me

yet! They still hold a wondrous surprise. As we reach the crest of the hill, the sun meets us, warming my face and caressing my shoulders. I have the impression that "God's in His heaven; all's right with the world," and I have a well-earned place of joy and potential to fulfill in that world.

Developing Senses

The most exciting part of my sensory adventure is that it is not necessary for me to share it with you simply as an author. Sensory possibility exists for each and every one of us. It is true that, because of my lack of sight, I have been forced to develop my remaining senses to a greater degree. But it is important to note the world "develop." I was not born with more acute senses. I had to develop them. Each of us has within himself the possibility to plug in, turn on, and turn up his sensory antennae, to submerge himself in new levels of joy and self-actualization.

The best examples I can give you for understanding the possibilities of development come from the ultimate innocence of little children, in this case my own. Blythe, my little girl, is nine; and Tommy, my son, is seven. They have enjoyed my world of sensory knowledge since they were babies. From the beginning of their communication, they had to learn to verbalize their feelings in order for me to understand what they felt. Consequently, sound became very critical in attaining their goals; a particular toy, food, or their need to be changed had to be expressed by sound. I can clearly remember the fact that they knew the difference between the times when Patty was with them and the times when I was performing my fatherly duties.

A Potpourri of Senses

When Blythe was about four and Tommy was two, we began to play what became a fun family game. The game was called "What's Mommy doing," and it started one evening when Patty was in the kitchen cooking dinner. I happened to ask Blythe what we were having, and she said she didn't know but she would go and look. I said, "No, don't go look; tell me by smelling it. What do you think we are having?" She had absolutely no idea; but I could clearly tell that it was the blood-red smell of a great roast beef and baking potatoes. And I heard the sound of Patty slicing fresh carrots and mixing up hollandaise sauce, probably for asparagus. I poured these things out to Blythe, and we began from that time on to use the evening meal as an educational process for sensory awareness.

This initial game generated others. Sitting in the backyard, I would make the children tell me all the things they could sense in the immediate area—the sounds of birds, the smell of flowers, the touch of autumn leaves, the taste of coming rain, the sound of traffic—all of these things became like old friends to

Blythe and Tommy; and they are better people for the experience. Tommy now loves the sound of a football or baseball game as much as he loves watching it. There is nothing like the pop of a ball in a glove, or the crack when it hits the bat, unless it's the thump of a well-kicked football, or the crash of helmets and shoulder pads when two adversaries come together.

Sensory Memories

When I was a little boy, I used to love the sound of my father shaving in the bathroom early in the morning but hated the sound of chalk on a blackboard. There is nothing like the feel and smell of clean, white, linen sheets when they've been hanging on a clothesline all day in the New England fall breeze. How about the smell of a wet-with-dew rose just before it opens or a lilac in full bloom? Does anything taste better than a juicy tomato just picked from the vine and eaten whole? Or what about more subtle things like the feel and sound of reeling in a fish, a lovely woman coming down a flight of stairs in a silk dress, swishing forward to quietly say she is ready to spend a wonderful evening together; the sincerity and innocence of children when they say simply, "I love you, Daddy."

And a fire—oh, I love a fire, crackling on a cold winter's day, when I am warmed by its warmth, soothed by its sound, comforted by its smell. The head of a newborn baby—what an incredible thing to touch, with its unblemished skin, so pure and smooth that it seems almost unreal—almost alabaster, yet it's warm and vital and so alive; the smell of that special child; I have never ever experienced anything so clean!

Did you ever taste a snowflake? It is so cold that it actually has no taste, nor does a cold winter have any particular smell, but you always know when it is here. The ground—the wonder of the ground on the first day of spring when the earth seems moist and promising. I'll never forget what it was like to grow up in New England and experience that first day, after the cold and emptiness of a winter without life.

Sensory Interaction

The fascinating thing, however, is that sensory awareness is not just aesthetic. It relates directly to our ability to interact with each other. Let me give you some concrete examples. Let's start with the most basic of our immediate contact—the handshake between two people who are just meeting for the first time. First, think of all the different kinds of hands you have shaken—not just the big or small hands, or the firm or delicate hands, but of each hand as having its own individual textures of hard work, creative arts, or exceptional vanity (usually noted in the nails), and along with those textures, the nuances or personality. There is the firm, quick handshake of the person giving you the impression that he is glad to see you, when you both know that he doesn't really care at all. Then there is the tentative handshake from a shy person, afraid of contact. There is the pumping, defined handshake of someone who is not only genuinely glad to see you, but is genuinely glad to be alive. There is the perspiring palm of a person who is concerned about an upcoming confrontation with you. There is the hesitant handshake, differing from the shy handshake of the person who was introduced to you even though he did not choose to be. All of this, and so much more, can be sensed, filed, and understood on just the immediate basis of a handshake.

We haven't even begun yet to talk about the auditory input. Do you know that a smile has a sound? It is very sibilant and very direct, and there is no lovelier sound. There is also no more depressing sound than that of a frown. It seems to come from a person whose head is down, and the voice half resonates from the chest rather than emanates from a person who is looking directly at you. There is the nervousness of rapid speech, or the attempt to try too hard with forced laughter, that usually rings very empty in dead air between two people wanting to get to know one another. There is the husky roundness of sensuality and romantic possibility; and the coldness that can so easily be put into a voice signaling "Leave me alone." There is the charm of persuasion, and the specialness of "I love you." There is the stuttering of indecision, and the power of positive process differing from the anger-aggression sound.

Think how far ahead you could be if you could use this data, particularly on the telephone. So often I have been fooled by people communicating on the phone who have given me the impression that they were not really anxious to see me; yet on meeting them, I found out that they were. Conversely, how many times has warmth been expressed over the phone without the directness of a meeting?

Physical Correlations

I have even been able to draw physical correlations to the human voice so that I could understand the appearance of others, particularly women. When I was going through my pimple-puberty stage and hoping that I could land a date for the junior prom, I began to notice that most of the young women who approached me were not particularly physically appealing. In later years, as I became an adult, that part of a person became less and less important. But during those years, it was vitally important to me that I be with an attractive young girl. I devised a method relating their sound to their appearance. Tall women, I decided, usually speak slowly and do everything more elegantly, accentuating the fact that they are tall. Dark-haired women seem to have lower speaking voices. Blondes seem to be overexposed to that old adage "blondes have more fun" and bubble on in rapid high-pitched speech. Women who are particularly well-endowed always talk out of rounded shoulders, because when they were in the seventh grade, they were concerned about being developed too early.

I expect now that you are all laughing, saying, "Isn't he amazing, learning to understand all those things." That is not what I want you to think. I want you to believe that the world of common senses is totally untapped by most people, that we live principally in our visual experience and have not even begun to expose ourselves to four other magnificent possibilities. Beauty is not just in the "eyes" of the beholder, it is in all the "common senses" of the beholder.

Labels

We have a habit of labeling anything we view as different. We do that in order to help ourselves pigeonhole people into convenient niches that make it easy for us not to get involved. We apply the limitation of what we see and the limitation of our language to define the level on which we are willing to participate and interact with others. And words, like *black, white, man, woman, old, young, blind, deaf,* and *retarded* permeate our view of each other. I believe that we can agree on a simple theorem: Sensory expansion will cause an evolution in human development. Human awareness will prompt tolerance, patience, understanding, and love. If you believe you *are* special, and that uniqueness can only be achieved through the application of common senses, you *are* special, because you have unlimited dimensions to utilize untapped, unsensitized tools, "common senses"—the simplest of all gifts, waiting just for you.

You Are Special

You *are special*. Such an easy thing to say. Three words that can take a lifetime to understand and put in motion, but three words that can change the course of a life any time you make the decision to positively assert that specialness. Through the uniqueness of being human, you hold the option of making changes at any time you choose.

All of us face the constant fear that we are failing in the determination of our own destiny; but that failure can be instantly changed by the decision to eradicate it. I do not want to mislead you though. The decision can be instant; but the process is daily, continuous, and never-ending. There is nothing quite as exciting as this daily battle of moving upward,

Tom, his wife, Patty, and their
children, Tommy and Blythe.

climbing the rungs of the ladder of your own specialness.

A Never-Ending Search

I have yet to meet a successful person who has retired early and found inner peace. I'm not suggesting that such people cannot be happy; but close examination of their lives shows that they have a compulsive need to achieve at something even when they seem to have finished with the confrontation of career and total goal orientation. Pursuits may have become more internalized, but their goals are just as important to them as they ever were. Consider the businessman who, at age fifty, has succeeded enough to leave corporate life. His golf game has probably moved from a twenty-two handicap to a twelve handicap, and he is still working to get that handicap down to an eight. Likewise, the woman who has raised her family is often more active in community projects than she ever was during the time her children were being raised. Priorities may change, but the quest never ends and, frankly, it never should.

You are special because there is no one exactly like you, and no one deals with the same complex human circumstances that you do. Although we obviously have similarities, our lifestyle, hopes, dreams, and failures hinge on the way in which we perceive ourselves in our particular set of circumstances.

A Positive Self-Image

A young man playing professional basketball with the Houston Rockets is a good example of how a person's perception of himself can shape his life. Calvin Murphy stands barely five feet, ten inches. Now that is not small, being only one and one-half inches below the American average of 1976. Calvin, however, plays a game in which the average height is six feet, seven and one-half inches—a game of giants. What made Calvin special? Persistence and the assertion of a positive self-image.

You will read about self-image again and again in this text, in different ways and mirrored in different case studies, but the evolvement of self-image must go hand in hand with the assertion of your own specialness. Calvin Murphy has been an NBA all-star four times, with a career average better than eighteen points a game, and has asserted himself as one of the premier stars of a highly competitive sport. Murphy is also an excellent businessman, a champion baton twirler (that is a sport far more complicated than it seems), and a person involved in community and social concerns.

These are the by-products of an evolving positive self-image. When positive specialness is asserted by any of us in a particular area, we find, for the most part, that it transforms itself into an entire lifestyle. The old adage of "ask a busy person and it will positively get done" is the truth. Positive self-perception translates directly to success, and that is the goal of all of us—to have an overriding sense of well-being, a constant belief in the ability to assert who we are in a world of competition, conflict, and compromise. Realistically, without positive self-assertion, our lives might as well be categorized as vacuums.

Though I believe that we are interested in the well-being of others, in the end whether *we* will actually succeed is clearly up to *us*. In the end, the alcoholic will be left in skid row by those who love him. The high school dropout will be forgotten about and will have to determine his or her own destiny alone. A person losing a loved one will be cared for by those who love him only for a time, and then must begin a new life. We are all totally individual and are forced to assert that individuality for ourselves. My greatest hope for my own children is that someday they will voluntarily choose to love me, believing that I am both their father and their friend.

A Self-Image Crisis

My marriage faced its most substantive crisis when I was forced to recognize that Patty's special-ness was being usurped by my own. Her sense of independence had turned to one of dependence, and she was being swallowed up by my selfishness. Had she not cried out, "I am me, and that's important!" I might never have listened, and she might never have become the person she is today. We now form a synergistic union. Our marriage is made up of the *you* person, the *me* person, and some kind of third entity which takes the best of who we are and is the governing force from which all decisions relating to our married lives seem to come. But first, we both had to adjust our lives to Patty's decision to assert her own specialness.

When Patty married a performer who must, in order to survive, have a huge and constantly starved ego, compounded by blindness which necessitated constant assurance, her survival as an individual was virtually impossible. It was only her faith and belief in some innate goodness she thought I must have inside that kept her hanging on for the first four years of our married lives. Not only did she have to be at my beck and call, but I didn't seem willing to allow relationships with people who might have become important to her. Our friends were my friends; my needs preempted any of hers. If I'd been working in some cheap nightclub during the week, I had no interest in getting out of the house with her for a very needed break on Sundays. The children were her children, not our children. I had no daily participation and was not involved in anything relating to their care. In effect, Patty not only had Blythe and Tommy to care for, but her husband, too. She had also to deal with my sense of her sexuality. I did not allow her to grow slowly; I expected her to be physically aggressive right from the beginning of our relationship, and it did not dawn on me that, for a woman, physical needs connect directly to emotional securities and self-assertion. How many men have been just like me? I shudder to think. So here we were, this self-possessed idiot matched up with a non-self-assertive, jelly-like personality.

As it usually does, our issue of emotional needs and confrontation came to a head over something extremely small and seemingly unimportant. I had been working at North Conway, New Hampshire, at a nightclub during ski season and was forced to spend six days in sub-zero weather, then, face a seven-hour bus trip home so I could spend at least one day a week on Cape Cod with Patty and the children. It was a horrible lifestyle, and on this particular night, as on all others, the tension was unbearable. Patty had driven two hours in a snow-storm, with two crying children, to pick me up at the Boston bus station. I had come home and collapsed in my rocking chair. And here I was, a lump of selfish humanity, disinterested in the children and totally unconcerned with Patty's need to feel fulfilled as a woman.

The snow had stopped falling, and Patty thought it would be terrific if we got a babysitter and had dinner at the only small French restaurant in the village. I not only said, "No" but went into a tirade about how she had the nerve expecting I could come home and feel like fun and games after a week of hard work with a bunch of drunks who spent my evenings asking me if I could sing "Melancholy Baby" or some other innocuous old standard.

For the first time, Patty stood up for herself, not loudly or obnoxiously, but quietly.

She put her hand on my hand, stopping my tirade, and said, "Tommy, I guess you just don't want to be married. You are so self-possessed, you really don't need anyone but yourself, do you?"

I was shocked. I was amazed that Patty had found the self-assertiveness to simply tell me that I needed a change. We walked outside and hiked through the snow along the beach that bordered our home. It was quite an experience in itself—wintertime on a beach. Nothing could be more bleak or awesome, and no emotion could be more confused or empty than what I was feeling at that moment. Here was Patty, the person I felt was absolutely contented within our relationship, telling me she was not contented at all, and I had no sense of her unhappiness. Yet here was that person telling me that I needed to change or get out of our marriage. *She* didn't really need *me*. *She* could assert *herself*.

It reminded me of the-mouse-that-roared syndrome, but it frightened me, too; and I found myself learning things about Patty that I never knew before. She had intense feelings of personal need and personal frustration; the only reason she had dealt with our lives as if she were my servant instead of my wife was that she truly loved me more than herself. At least in the beginning she had felt that way, but now that self, that specialness, was crying out to be asserted and she couldn't stop it anymore. I was faced with the reality of either recognizing her specialness and accepting it or throwing it away and isolating myself in my own selfishness. Thank God I chose to listen to her. Thank God I chose to make the relationship count. Thank you, God, for letting me spend the rest of my life with Patty.

Since that confrontation on a winter's evening in the snows of Cape Cod, Patty has asserted her own specialness. It has made our relationship blossom into something more solid than any material item, more solid than anything nature can contrive, because love is the most solid, intact, wondrous material of human emotion; its fibers can be stretched but never broken. Over the last few years, Patty has been on a rampage of self-assertion, from teaching to tennis. She is totally involved in my work, no longer as a surrogate worker but as an equal partner with exciting ideas and contributions. She is even a better mother, relishing the achievements of our children. She is all those things because she has asserted her own specialness, because she is celebrating her own uniqueness, and because she has found a positive outlet for the involvement of self-image. In effect, she is living, really living.

A Person Is Special—Anytime

Patty asserted her specialness as a young adult, but the realization that a person is special can come at any time in life. Someone else I love very much, my mother, began asserting herself later in life, but just as successfully. My mother was born in 1912 and is now sixty-eight years old. For the majority of her adult life, she lived in a situation in which she was totally taken care of. That is not to say she did not have massive responsibilities, but in the mentality of the 1930s, a man was truly the head of the household, and it was the woman's job to keep the family structure in order—that was all. Consequently, women rarely held jobs or took responsibility for anything dealing with the finances of the home.

In my mother's case, my father gained affluence as the years went by, and my mother was the "belle of the ball." Everyone loved them; everyone had to have Marie and Tom Sullivan as guests at their party. In short, my mother never had to take any worldly responsibility or assert her own place in the order of things. In later years, through a set of exceptionally sad circumstances, my mother and father ended their marriage. Since the children were grown, there was no support for my mother, and she was placed in a situation in which she had to fend for herself, even selling her house, an exceptionally difficult decision for her. I don't think I yet understand how intensely difficult that time was; not only was the home being sold, but a large part of my mother's self-image was going with it.

She was forced to revamp her entire life. No longer were the bills paid or the groceries purchased by someone else. No longer could she simply go to the store and buy the things she needed with no regard for their payment. No longer were there leisurely shopping trips and charge cards to fill her time. Her "dance card" now consisted of absolutely basic subsistence: the necessity of social security and the awareness of imposed financial restrictions. I remember she said to me once that she had never written a check in her life until three years earlier.

Somehow, through the determination of the human spirit, my mother has not only survived, but flourished. She has done everything from balance her checkbook to learn to drive. There are still problems facing her, the question of housing and the future—problems so prevalent among senior citizens in America today. I believe, however, that with just a little help from the rest of the family, she will find ways to succeed.

Far more substantive than even these physical considerations were the emotional changes. My mother has become an interesting and outgoing human being, phenomenally involved in the interaction of all the people she loves and finally able to establish friendships on her own. She is involved in everything from league bowling to bingo games with people she had never met. Like Patty, my mother has finally asserted herself in an overall social scheme of things.

I'm tremendously proud of her ability to establish her own uniqueness, to realize that she still has contributions to make and that life holds for her the exciting possibility of new and daily explorations. I'm sure that she is becoming far more special now than she thought she was before. The daily challenges of survival have enhanced the development of her own self-image. She is a classic example of the evolution of specialness. She proves that it can occur at any time and that all of us hold the right, the absolute right of personal choice.

You are special; believe it. You are special; celebrate it. You are special because I am convinced that I am special, and we are not that different. We must make the same decisions and come to the same resolves. Learn to love and appreciate your specialness, for you are, indeed, special.

Who Am I?

Who am I? I'm Tom Sullivan, and I believe that is important. I believe it is the most important thing I know. I believe that I am special, and that specialness is something that I am still struggling to understand. That specialness is allowing me to bridge the gap of loneliness, to keep from falling into the canyons of self-pity, to climb the mountain range of life's goals, to travel over the seemingly endless oceans of misunderstanding, to navigate the waves of anger, and finally, to touch the islands of love and friendship. All of this is made possible because I am special.

This ultimately elusive truth, so much like mercury, a quicksilver in my mind, slipping through the consciousness again and again, came to me gradually

The author in a thoughtful moment.

and still may elude my very being without hard, consistent discipline and the absolute, positive belief in my own uniqueness. I am attempting, therefore, to celebrate my own uniqueness, relishing who I am, and, on that basis, to appreciate the uniqueness of others.

It is in the uniqueness of others that we find our own specialness, mirrored in how they perceive us. There is no effort here to play mental gymnastics or look for subliminal essence; in these next pages, it is my hope to clearly define both my own uniqueness and the uniqueness that I seek and find in others. It seems too easy to discuss, essay, and pronounce this kind of truth now; but as a young blind child, I was as far away from understanding and enjoying life as a space traveler headed for the outer-limits of the galaxy. How we see ourselves and how others see us is a constant tug-of-war with self-identity and self-esteem.

A Negative Self-Image

In my own case, the early loneliness imposed on me because of blindness nurtured a highly negative self-image. My early childhood was filled with anger and self-pity. The first time I can remember becoming aware that I was viewed as different was on a sunny, spring afternoon in my backyard in West Roxbury, Massachusetts.

My mother and father had decided that the best

thing they could do for their blind son was to isolate him in a very safe, secure fenced-in backyard. Down the street from my house, there was a little league baseball field where an exciting game was in progress. I sat on my swing and could hear the sound of the baseball hitting the bat and the excited cries of the young players doing their best to become the next Tom Seaver or Pete Rose, and I desperately wanted to be a part of their game. That was impossible, and I guess even in my early stage of growth I knew. But that didn't mean that I couldn't imagine myself a part of their's or anyone else's game.

My father had given me a little league bat and I constantly carried it around. And on this spring day, I decided that I could start my own game. My yard was half grass and half pebbles, and I started to pick up small rocks, realizing that if I held the rocks in my left hand and the bat in my right, I could, with luck, make contact between bat and rock. I knew it wasn't the best thing for the bat, but I so desperately needed to feel the contact with others and the things they did that I guess I decided breaking my baseball bat had some validity. So, to the cries of the little boys playing baseball down the street, I began to imitate the game. When they would hit the baseball, sending it somewhere into the little league outfield, I would hit my rock and imagine myself circling the bases to the screams and cheers of my teammates. By the way, I did this with whatever sport happened to be in season. For example, during football, I would run around my own yard, knocking myself down and cheering as if I were running for a touchdown, again duplicating the sounds I heard.

But back to baseball. I was in the middle of the ninth inning in one of my make-believe games on this particular afternoon when a little boy came by my fence. He confronted me with his sense, his reality, as to who I was. He looked through the fence and he saw me carrying out my make-believe game and said, "How you doing, Blindey?"

The word "Blindey" was applied to me for the first time in my consciousness. It didn't seem too bad when he first said it. It didn't hurt too much, but the tone of his voice was a tone that I came to know very well, a tone that represented ridicule or patronage, pity or passive disinterest, superiority or amazement—and all of these words pointing toward "difference." Difference, that meant dependence, helplessness, alienation, complete social misunderstanding. Difference—a word I learned to hate, learned to use, and at times abuse for my own advantage.

But to the little boy in the backyard, it just meant "What are you doing, Blindey?" A statement, a question asked by a child who simply didn't know what I was doing or why I was doing it. And I was too young, and certainly not articulate enough, to be able to explain to him that what I was doing was trying to be a part of life, trying to relate, trying to share. All I could do was throw my bat down and run into my house, hoping my mother could help me understand the reality of my own "inconvenience."

I've since come to think about blindness as an inconvenience, not a handicap. All of us happen to have handicaps. Some may be a great deal more subtle than my obvious physical one, but each one of us has to make the same decision to take that handicap and turn it into only an inconvenience. This premise, however, took me years to understand; and in this first confrontation with reality, all I felt was emptiness, loneliness, and the beginnings of an anger that worked to my advantage as the years went by.

So I asked my mother what the little boy meant when he said, "Hi, Blindey." My mother found it impossible to confront me with the truth, to tell me that the little boy was just curious and wasn't really ridiculing me. He only knew me by my label, "Blindey." What she chose to say was that he was being mean, and that he didn't understand, and that he was a bad little boy. And I took that to mean that I was to dislike him. I didn't want to dislike him; I wanted to play with him.

Somewhere in my child's brain—in my childhood experience—I formulated the belief that the only way I could play with others was to be better at things than they were, that in order to be equal, I had to be superior. I spent most of the next fifteen years living in a world of high pressure, overextended goals, highly stressed self-image, attempting to attain impossibilities, attempting to turn the world upside down, changing it to allow me to be a part of it. I learned that none of us is an earthshaker. We are all just looking for a place to keep both feet on the ground and be recognized as special.

The Quest for Equality

One of the first thoughts confronting me as I began to mature was to wonder what I had to share, what talent I could employ to be equal. While I was pondering this, summer turned to winter, and my first chance to participate as an equal with sighted children occurred because of an accident of nature. I was again in my backyard, only this time it was covered with a foot of New England snow. I was wrapped up in a winter ski jacket with heavy boots, trying like any other kid to manufacture a snowman, when I heard the sound of those same little boys, not playing baseball, but discussing who had the guts to jump off my next-door neighbor's house roof into snowdrifts. I remember thinking just for a split second, "How high is a roof?" but that thought was quickly put aside by my own need to feel that I could join them. And so I yelled very loudly, "I'll do it! I'll do it!" One of them heard me. I heard him say, "The blind kid said he would do it." Tommy would jump off the roof of the house.

So four little boys let me out of the yard (Thank goodness my mother wasn't watching!) and took me, like a gladiator going off to war, up on top of the house roof. Now the reality sunk in. I was high up in the air. At least a sighted person can look down and come up with some perspective. For a blind person, it's like standing on the edge of oblivion waiting to fall into an endless abyss. All the thoughts of my young life seemed to flash through my mind. Did I really want to do this? Did I really want to put my life out in space, dangling it there just so I could play with the boys next door?

Well, I didn't wait long to make the decision. Somehow I got the courage and lunged into space. In retrospect, I realize the fall was probably about eight feet, and when I hit the cushion of new-fallen snow, the cheers from the little boys were the greatest sounds I had ever heard in my young life. Before I even had a chance to crawl out of the snowdrift, four other bodies had landed in it next to me and a union was begun. Billy and Mike Hannon and John and David Turnbull became my weekend friends—"weekend" because my parents had decided that I should attend a school for the blind, a school that ultimately isolated me and kept me from being a part of life as it really was.

I've come to understand over the years that there are, of course, specific educational needs handicapped children have, and on that basis, require special help;

but none of us as a human being can afford to be isolated from integral social contact with others. Any educational system that fosters this belief is doing far more to damage its students than to help them. Even with these new-formed friendships, however, life hadn't yet turned the corner. No matter what the game was, I was always the last person chosen for the team, the person that nobody really wanted on his side but had to take because, well, because I was there.

Try to understand the dichotomy. During the week, I attended the school for the blind, and I was the best at everything—the first person on the team—the captain of many of the teams, as it were. Then to come home on weekends and feel the social ostracism from some of the kids in the neighborhood who really didn't know me seemed to be more than I could handle. The only alternative was to find some vehicle, some form of expression in which I could be a winner—not necessarily jumping off the roof into snowdrifts or going into the neighborhood haunted house saying that since I was blind, I couldn't see the ghost anyway—but some clear-cut activity in which I could compete directly.

One of the only integrated, social activities that was a part of life within the school for the blind was wrestling. Thank God for it. As I look back, I can't say that I ever really loved the sport. It became my obsession because I was willing to compete on an equal basis with sighted young men though, I must admit, my start could not be considered auspicious. In my first three matches, my total time on the mat was less than one minute. I would walk out, shake hands nervously, the referee would blow his whistle, and before I knew it, I was flat on my back on the mat with the referee's hand slapping it, telling me that I'd lost. To say that I was crushed would be a graphic understatement.

In my fourth match, the coach told me that I had no chance to win. He said that the boy I was competing against was a leading candidate for the New England championships that year, but it would be a valuable experience if I were able to relax and stay in the match for a while. I remember that my mother and father were there that day, and I told them that I would probably quit after this match. I was so depressed, but I decided to give it one more terrific effort, expecting to lose.

When the match began, I was less tense than before and my body seemed to function with more fluidness. Surprisingly, I survived the first onslaught and by the end of the first period, though I was behind two to nothing, I was still competing. In the second period, I was able to gain what was called a "reversal," transferring myself from the bottom position to the top, consequently tying the score. The referee blew his whistle at the end of the second period. I was exhausted but beginning to feel elation.

In high school wrestling a player is allowed to communicate for one minute between the second and third periods with his coach, and I don't think Dick Kamus believed it. He said, "Sullivan, I can't believe you are still out there; I can't believe you are still participating, but you have a chance to win this match. Now go out and do something!"

I couldn't wait for the whistle to begin the third period. I seemed to find new energy, as underdogs often do. And as the period went on, I began to feel my opponent's body weaken. He was on his stomach, and I was applying a half nelson (a hold used like a crowbar to pry the opponent from the stomach position over onto his back). I was amazed! His body was beginning to turn. Then he was on his back and my hands were tightening around his neck, my body crushing him down, straining to hold him as he bridged, lifting his body from the pinning position. But somehow I felt a new strength and maybe a new purpose. And when the referee's hand came down that day, it was not announcing my defeat, but my first victory—an unbelievable experience!

This victory was really over the world as I saw it, not just my opponent; and of all the achievements which have occurred since, it was certainly the most personally fulfilling. I was very fortunate to go on and win over three hundred more matches in my wrestling career and to achieve two national championships. I was also fortunate to have been blessed with the physical talent that enabled me ultimately to accomplish this feat. But I believe that to a greater or lesser degree, each one of us clearly has "a talent" that we can be proud of, a talent that will help us achieve success—maybe not success as viewed by others, but success that is important to us: the celebration of our own uniqueness and a sense of our own specialness.

Along with wrestling, my musical horizons were expanding. I was the soloist in the glee club, a leader in the school band; and on weekends I had the chance to earn money by singing Irish songs in my father's nightclub. Coupling this with the normal overgrown ego of a high school senior, I realize in reflection that my self-confidence was ballooning out of control.

My need to constantly reaffirm the fact that I was equal became overwhelming to everyone around me. If I were to go to a party, for example, I would somehow turn the conversation around to the things that I was doing to point out to everyone that blind people could do anything they could do and probably do it better. Consequently, my friendships were limited, and people's views of me were not based on their liking me, but based on all the extremes of feeling sorry for me or believing that I was superior or some kind of freak of nature. I fueled this image, not just by guiding conversations toward things I was doing, but by taking advantage of my inconvenience.

In my first international wrestling meet against a boy from the Soviet Union, I was losing eleven to one midway in the second period. I must say that he was without question a superior athlete, and I was finding it impossible to compete with him on an equal basis. I decided in a moment of great pain that there was only one thing to do. I had to find a different way to win. I happen to have prosthetic (plastic) eyes, so the next time he knocked me down, grinding my head into the mat, I somehow maneuvered one of my plastic eyes out and screamed, "Stop! Stop!" Thank goodness, he at least understood that word because he did relax and look down. I screamed, "I lost my eye!" And upon seeing the plastic blob right under his nose, he immediately gagged and was forced to withdraw from the match.

At this point in life I'm not proud of that behavior. And it was this kind of taking advantage of a situation that may have alienated me from some friends that I might have had, but the incident does illustrate how all of us must learn how to turn adversity into advantage. There are a number of ways to do this. We can simply practice to become better at the things that we do not do well. We can avoid participating in things which might make our disadvantage more obvious. Or we can develop a sense of humor—not laughing *at ourselves*, but *about* our *situation*. My life turned around when I realized that Tom Sullivan wasn't funny, but that things relating to his inconvenience were hysterical.

A New Point of View

Two stories from my early college life will illustrate the point quite well. In 1967 I was attending Providence College in Rhode Island. On a night in mid-autumn the campus was plunged into darkness due to a power blackout all over the New England and northeast area. Our portable radios were afire with excited newsmen conjecturing as to whether our situation was caused by the Russians finding a new way of carrying out the cold war, the Chinese deciding that the Maoist revolution should spread quickly west, or the other minorities—blacks, Jews, Chicanos—rising up. One commentator even entertained the idea of a possible invasion from outer space. I decided at that moment not only to put some levity into the situation, but to score a point for my own uniqueness with the student body on the Providence College campus. Finding a portable megaphone used by cheerleaders supporting the Friar's Basketball team, I climbed atop of Harkins Hall, the main academic building, and announced that though people might think it was a Russian or Chinese plot that threatened the present security, it was actually the first maneuver of take-over by the country's most forgotten and suppressed minority of all—the blind—and the gentlemen of the Providence College Student Body would be getting their instructions from their blind coordinator momentarily.

As it was the dinner hour and after dark, I climbed down from my distinguished podium and forced my fellow students to line up, holding onto each other's pants in order to find out where they were going; and I led my procession to the candle-lit cafeteria for supper. What a moment of personal gratification! I will never forget it! It clearly changed the course of the way I looked at my inconvenience. I was able not only to strive for my own specialness, but to take myself less seriously, not forcing participation in every human event as if it were a matter of life or death.

The second story illustrates the changeover even more graphically. It deals with my ability to finally allow someone else to make a joke about me. I had the chance in my first two years of college to share a room with a guy named Tom Slye. Slye was never referred to as a Robert Redford-look-alike, but to me he was the most beautiful soul I've ever known. Anyway, in our two years of common address, his main joy was in finding things about our situation that he viewed as comical. One morning I was getting dressed—a function that I had been carrying out successfully for years. Tom entered the room and watched me for a time, taking note of my progress. I guess I had gotten into my shirt and pants, and as I began putting on my socks, he interrupted me.

"What are you doing?' he said.

"What do you think I'm doing? I'm getting dressed."

He looked at me for a moment and said, "Tom, we've been roommates for a year and a half now, and you know how much I care about you. This is a sensitive area, but I feel it's my duty as your friend to tell you something before you graduate from college and head for the big leagues. You know that there is a left and right shirt sleeve?"

"Yes, " I agreed.

"And that there is a left and a right pantleg? And a left and a right shoe?"

"Yes."

"Well, Tom, when you put on your socks, there's a left and a right sock."

"What do you mean?" I snapped. "That's impossible! There couldn't be! I would have known that by this time." But my own insecurity began to emerge, bubbling to the surface, and I had to say to him, "Well, how do you know?"

He absolutely had me then. He said, "Well, one is tighter than the other."

I repeated questioningly, "Tighter?"

He said, "Yes! You'd be able to tell if you practice, because one is definitely tighter."

I said, "I guess that makes sense. One foot is usually slighter larger than the other. I mean, I kick the football with my right foot; it's the foot that I always use to step down. It probably does have greater muscular development."

For the next week, every morning, this miserable human being would enter our room and watch me dress, discussing in detail the significance of a left and a right sock. Suffice it to say for the purpose of this chapter, I eventually caught on to this one-sided humor and learned the truth, which began a lifelong rampage of revenge against my tall, skinny friend. The point is, he allowed me to gain access to one of the great secrets of finding my own specialness. And that is the ability to laugh, not at myself, but about my situation.

One would think, then, that I had life pretty well in hand. I mean, I'd achieved physical success through the wrestling; my musical talent was beginning to emerge and grow; and I had found a relationship with a true and honest friend. But I was still struggling too hard. I had not yet learned to celebrate the uniqueness of others. I was so caught up in my own ego and its needs that I didn't seem to be concerned about the plight of others. I didn't seem to need to empathize with who they were. To put it as directly as possible, I was simply a selfish college brat, and as I became more successful, I became more egotistical.

I guess it has to do with overcompensation. My own quest for self-image had made me interested in only one image. At times I am frankly amazed that I had any friends at all. To really be special is to achieve uniqueness without having to force it upon others. I hope this book will let the people I knew during those periods realize that, even though I functioned immaturely, it came out of the burning desire to be equal.

It is amazing that during that growing process I did not lose my life. I made thirty-nine jumps out of airplanes, drove motorcycles, peddled a bike off a thirty-foot pier just to show I could ride a two-wheeler, was hit in the head by every conceivable kind of ball, had twenty-one concussions received in unique experiences like running into trees, skating into the side of a hockey arena, water-skiing into a dock, and on and on and on. But the fates have allowed me to survive, and brought me to a place of contentment and valuable self-image.

Certainly, the people contributing most to that process have been my wife, Patty, and my two children, Blythe and Tommy. Patty chose to love a person not at face value, but on the basis of the person she felt was inside—the person I had the potential to become. I hope she's right. She modified the anger, changed the bitterness to compassion, and supported every activity in my quest for identification. In their innocence, my children have made me aware that for them I am simply their father. They came to this life with no preconceived notions about either themselves or the people who surround them with love.

It's wonderful for me to recall some of the things

they have said. One afternoon while playing baseball with my little boy—a game that puts my life in jeopardy every time he winds up and throws—I was hitting the ball to him for fielding practice. In the excitement of the game, I changed my own direction, hitting the ball far to his left. He had to run a long way to get it; and when he brought it back, I found myself saying to my seven-year-old, "I'm sorry, Tom, maybe you would have been better off having a father who could really play with you."

My little boy looked up with simply an open framework of concern and said, "Gee, Dad, you don't have to say you're sorry when you play with me." What perspective!

He was also playing football with me one day and made me laugh about the simple problem he experienced by having to do too much in the game to make it interesting. I'm thirty-two years old, and in all of my previous football experience I had been designated as the center. The idea was, let the blind kid hike the ball and block a tree, which, by the way, I did once. I'll never forget my father coming to the hospital asking me how I felt. The only thing I could think of to tell him was, "How come they let the big kid play?" Well, anyway, Tommy and I decided to go out into the backyard and have our own brand of NFL football. For the first time in my life, I was going to be the quarterback—a very special experience when you've never had that opportunity. Tommy had put on his football uniform—Ram shirt, helmet, shoulder pads and cleats—and I expected the game to last at least an hour. After five minutes, Tommy brought me the ball and said, "I quit, Dad."

"Why?" I said.

"Look, Dad, when you throw the ball, I catch it. When I throw the ball, I have to go get it, so I quit." At that moment, all I could do was commend my child for his honesty.

My little girl was playing with a friend and the friend said, "Blythe, is your daddy blind?"

"Yes," said Blythe.

The little friend said, "What does blind really mean?" Blythe responded, "Blind means that Daddy can't see, but God taught him other stuff."

I think she was right. I'm so glad she was right. And I believe my major contribution in life is the guidance and continued well-being of those children, watching them fulfill themselves, becoming all they can be.

For those of you who don't know, I have spent the greater part of the last ten years in a sometimes frustrating, but also very fulfilling, pursuit of musical success which has included everything from writing music to making records, giving concerts and even making a few movies now and then. I have had the good fortune to spend time with people from all walks of life in many parts of the world, and I am fascinated and sometimes frightened by the impact that one in this profession can have on large numbers of people. For myself, I can only hope that at those times in my life I can effect positive change.

I mention the show-business industry because, possibly more than in any other profession, one must be able to deal with the (airplane ride!) peaks and valleys of a business with no security. Under these circumstances most of us could easily fall into depression—that horrible sense that there is nothing we can do about our situation. We allow ourselves to be crushed by what *has* happened. It is significant to note that depression is based on what has *passed*, not on the moment at hand, for that moment is an open and independent chance to move toward something far more significant. It is not only possible, it is essential to live every day of our lives with gusto.

I believe that my circumstances have forced me to make the most of each opportunity that life has held out, and I have just begun to achieve the most that is possible within the focus of each moment. I am, then, finally satisfied with who I am. That does not mean that I am satisfied with who I will become; that joyous quest is still in front of me. But I am content that I have evolved into someone who can continue the challenge for success, who will achieve most of his goals, and who can enjoy all that life has to offer.

My life is an experiment, a study, in what is possible. I have learned to take adversity and turn it into advantage. I have forced people to drop the label of "handicapped," which so often pigeonholed me, and turn it into "inconvenienced," which means only that I must find another way to do the same job. I have finally found that personal level of equilibrium —a relative sense of harmony—with my life as it is and the future to come.

I've learned that dependence is incomprehensible and independence is impossible; that there must be some level called "interdependence." I've learned that pity can never be accepted and that uncompromising stubbornness is just as dangerous, that potential only counts if it becomes actualized participation, that everyone has particular gifts to offer if he is willing to search for them.

Life is so rich it must be pursued to the limits of human possibility. I hope that I have not given the impression that this process is easy. It is not. It is fraught with pitfalls and, frankly, most of us only get part way up the mountain. It is the climbing of that mountain that counts, not the achievement of the pinnacle. We must learn to find happiness in the day to day process of life's climb.

In my own life, I believed that the only way to survive was to compete directly against someone else. That is how I would achieve equality. I have learned in time that the only major competition that counts is the one you carry out against yourself; that you must evolve your own best yardstick. You must determine what is possible for you. You must decide what your goals are. You must decide where your limits fall. And you must decide what choices you are going to make.

I have recently become a distance runner; and as I sit here writing these pages, I am in the middle of training to run a marathon—twenty-six miles, three hundred and sixty-five yards. Most good runners would agree that when the body is pushed to its limits, the competition is squarely in your own head. And that is the way it should be.

We were put here as individuals, unique unto ourselves—God's greatest creation. He meant us to find our own way, to follow our own path. I hope that what I have to say in this book will act as helpful guideposts for possibility. There is no universal formula. There is only personal recommendation, and that recommendation is given out of a sincere concern for each person who reads this. We are bound together by the circumstances of being human. We will only choose to be together when we come to understand the specialness of each other. These pages are devoted to that issue. It is not my hope that you, as the reader, see this work as a testimony to the specialness of Tom Sullivan but as an example of one person's quest for his own uniqueness.

This is also not a biography. It is a personal view of my own interaction with other special people. If anything, it is a celebration of their specialness. It is also selfish. I want every reader to want to become special, so that the lifestyle for Patty, myself, and, most importantly, my children may be a better one as time marches on. You are special. Celebrate your own uniqueness. Become all you want to be. That is the Tom Sullivan Doctrine of Specialness. In the pages to follow, you will read it expressed in different ways over and over and over again. It represents the one truth that I am absolutely committed to, the one that I am absolutely sure of, the one that can allow you to reach higher than you ever expected, to examine a possibility, then make it a probability, then accomplish it, and then, wonder of wonders, move on to another, even more exciting possibility.

Turning Points

I believe there are moments in our lives that shape, dominate, and control our destiny. Within each, we hold options—options that make it possible for us either to move forward and upward in the spiral of mental, physical, and emotional evolution or to fall back into pits of depression, despair, and dependence. I don't think any of us can honestly look at our lives without being able to recognize our own particular turning points. I think we can look to these turning points as clear-cut barometers for answering the question, "Did we move toward positive life-involvement when confronting these choices?" The writing of this chapter has caused me to recollect my own turning points. Frankly, I'm not sure the choices I

Tom enjoying a horseback ride.

made were the correct ones, but I do know where and when these turning points occurred within my own human cycle, and discussing them openly may be of some help in recognizing your own moments of truth and decisions made about them.

An Early Turning Point

My first turning point came when I was about ten years old and went on a fishing trip with my father and some of his Boston Irish drinking buddies. My father was in the nightclub business during my early years. He was somewhat of a legend. In his lifetime he had been a prizefighter, a bootlegger for a very prominent family, an office boy for the *Atlantic Monthly* magazine, a professional wrestler, a record-holding amateur swimmer, a millionaire three different times, and a boisterous, heavy-drinking Irishman from his head to his toes. Suffice it to say that he was special. And even though the years and individual growing pains have weighed heavily on our relationship, he was the most charismatic force in my young life. Those wondrous moments when my father, his friends, and I went on fishing trips represented the highlights in my life.

As the beer and whiskey flowed, the fish never got larger but the stories did. I used to love to listen to my father, along with a couple of ex-politicians and the chief of police, recount the times they had shared along with the larger moments that made up the character of every Irishman—his personal and public legend—the expression of his manhood in story. On this particular day, we had started out early in the morning. The fishing had been terrific; and even my father, who normally never enjoyed the fishing, had caught six big cod and was in high spirits.

My best friend on these trips was the owner of the boat, a wonderful man to whom I owe so much, Tom McDonough. Tom was the only true fisherman on board; and on many other days he would take me out alone to fish for blues and bass—fish that the other men just didn't have the patience to trawl for. The goal for them was to get offshore a few miles, find some deep water, anchor, drop their lines, drink a lot of beer, tell a lot of stories, and let the line bob around until some big, lazy cod or flounder decided it was hungry. Then they would haul it up, throw it in the bucket, bring it home, clean, cook, and eat it and tell their wives what a terrific fight they had getting the Friday night dinner to the table.

At any rate, fishing had been extraordinarily good; and as the day wore on, none of us were aware of the incredible New England fog that was engulfing everything in its path, including a boat of drunken fishermen. McDonough was the first person to recognize it. He turned to my father and said, "Hey, Tom, we'd better pull up anchor and get in. If this stuff keeps rolling in, it'll be thicker than soup and we may be forced to stay out here longer than we'd like."

My father replied, typically, "Ah, bull, Mc-Donough! Open up another beer and relax. We're only a few miles off shore. I could swim that far."

My father was one of those men who made definitive statements even when he wasn't sure. The "few miles" were actually eight miles, as I was to find out in later years. But everything seems much closer when a person is looking over water. By the time McDonough filed his second complaint, though, even my father had to concede. He could no longer see his nose in front of his face, and what had been a fun, relaxing day now took on ominous seriousness.

The reason for the concern of the men, however, was not the fact that we all might end up spending the night at sea. McDonough's boat was more than safe; and, since it was mid-July, the temperature was warm enough for our survival. The issue confronting us was that Scituate was on a direct line with the Boston Harbor oceangoing ships, and those freighters burrowed through the waves with little regard for any insignificant fishing boats that might be in their paths. Though blarney and machismo dominated the characters of the men who were on the boat that evening, there was an undercurrent of real fear—fear of the unknown quantities that the ocean could churn up, man-made or otherwise.

The drinking ceased and gave way to the discussion of what we were going to do. Since at that time boat safety had not yet evolved as a requirement to allow one to take a craft out on the ocean, McDonough's fishing boat was not equipped with either radio or flares, so direct communication was eliminated. For awhile, we entertained the thought that a Coast Guard cutter might appear on its nightly patrol and tow us to safe harbor. But as darkness set in, we came to realize that that was not going to happen.

The wind, that had been blowing warm and southwesterly throughout the day, changed directions, turning cold—a sign for potentially stormy weather. By now the discussions had stopped, and all of us seemed to be transfixed, waiting for whatever the next moments would unfold. McDonough was still sitting at the wheel, his head in his hands, as I joined him. Standing next to him, my head just barely cleared the top of the windshield, but enough to have an unobstructed view, or sound-sense, of what was in front of us across the bleak open ocean.

Evening was turning to night. Even the wildly chirping birds had concluded their search for food for the day. Everything was totally quiet except for a sound that I could just barely hear, drifting toward me through the night on the northeast breeze. In the beginning I wasn't sure what it was. But as I listened more intently, the sound became quite familiar, something that was a part of all the fishing trips with Tom McDonough. It was the waves breaking against the bell buoy, marking the entrance to Scituate harbor far off in the distance.

"Can you hear it?" I said to McDonough.

"Hear what, Tommy?"

"The sound of the bell buoy. It's out there."

"No, I can't hear it," said McDonough. "I can't hear it at all. Hey, everybody, can you hear the bell buoy ringing out there in the night?"

The "No" was collective, but I knew I could hear it. My father rushed forward and said, "Tommy, could you guide us toward that sound? I mean, could you tell us if we were going toward it or if we moved to the right or left side of it?"

"I think so, Dad. I think I could."

"McDonough! Don't you understand?" my father said. "This is an open channel. There's nothing but small obstacle buoys out here. If we go slowly, even if we hit one, it won't damage the boat. And if Tom can keep us on line to the sound of that buoy, the harbor is just beyond it."

"All right," said McDonough. "Let's do it."

For the next three hours, the boat slowly made its way through the fog, with my helping to keep us on course by straining to listen to the buoy and keeping it in line with the end of my nose. I did so well that we almost ran directly into it, and would have had McDonough not seen the harbor lights.

To say my father was proud would be an understatement. For years afterward he spoke of his heroic son and the fact that his blindness had made him able to hear something that sighted people would have missed.

What my father said was true, and it marked the first critical turning point of my life. As I lay in bed that night, reveling in my accomplishment, my father came in and stood next to me. Holding my hands, he said, "Tommy, you're special. You saved our lives. I love you."

I couldn't doze off right away after my father left. I kept thinking of what he had said, and I kept thinking of how often I had wanted to be special, how often I had felt like the last person on earth who could be. My choices were obvious. I could take this experience and remember it as one fleeting moment of individual glory, or I could begin to assert myself with positive attitudes and actions. Somehow, in my young mind I determined to do just that. I decided that never again would I allow my blindness to be anything but an advantage, never again would I allow the limitation of my self-image to restrict my participation in life. And I decided on that day to channel my other talents into evolving an exciting and personally rewarding lifestyle. I was on the way. I had come to my first major turning point and had molded it into a positive reinforcement for who and what I wanted to be.

Call it fate, coincidence; call it accident; call it design; call it whatever you like; but at that moment in time, Tom Sullivan had made an ultimately positive decision to believe in himself. I decided to believe that out of adversity can come strength; out of moments of truth can come lifetimes of successes; out of positive use of God-given talents can come satisfaction. I don't want to indicate here that what is being discussed represents some panacea, some immediate formula for finding Nirvana. I believe there are too many books and articles devoted to "methods" of spiritual salvation. I am sure, however, that what I am positing in these pages represents the simplest common denominator that binds us together in our struggle for personal goals; and it is to recognize who we are within our situations. This struggle for equilibrium among the forces pulling at us is continuous, and we never really win. If we did, there would be no joy in the struggle; and none of us, to use an old axiom, ever sees himself as others see him. We need someone else's perspective to help us recognize our turning points and our own specialness.

A Romantic Turning Point

Within the scope of my own knowledge there are no words that can clearly describe the depth or impact that my wife, Patty, has had on my life. Call this writer's license or personal strokes, or the utilization of cliches, but I would not be the person I am today without her. She is a stabilizing force in my life who is gentle and sensitive and at the same time organized and direct. She is poised without being prissy; she gives the impression of being happy in her life and tells people that without making them feel uncomfortable. Patty is also a phenomenal mother, willing to love as much as correct, and her voice has that special sound that glitters with a smile. Of all the special people I have met, to me, Patty is unique.

My next turning point came when I developed the ability to understand Patty's specialness. We had met in the most romantic of all circumstances—a carefree summer on the beaches of Cape Cod. The problem was that I was at a point in my life when I was looking forward to spending my nights under the moonlight with a great number of ladies; and for the first part of the summer I did just that. I used every strategy in an attempt to gain their compassion or pity through my blindness. What a horrible human being! Another wondrous advantage in meeting all the lovely young women during that summer was that it was my first time working as a performer.

I was singing at what was to become Cape Cod's "in" spot that summer. It was on one of those nights that the other half of my duo noted that two exceptionally attractive young women had entered the room. One was blonde, medium-size, with a lovely, tanned face. The other was tall, ravishingly well-endowed and seemed the type that would have a few drinks and a good time at a party or two. On my next break, I asked the young ladies if I could buy them a drink. They accepted my offer, and we sat down at a corner table and became acquainted. Being very partial to tall brunettes, I had very little to say to the short blonde, but I used every device from humor to sympathy to gain the attentions of Patty's friend, Connie, but had no luck at all. As they say, "she wasn't buying my act." I did get them to consent to join me the next day for a picnic on the beach—with them bringing the picnic, of course—which I considered a major victory. I didn't realize that it was Patty's swift kick under the table that convinced Connie to attend the picnic.

As it turned out, the next day when their old clunker car, affectionately called "the beast," pulled up in front of where I was living, Patty was the only one in it. I tried to hide my disappointment, but probably didn't do it very well. It is amazing how first impressions can melt away, and that was what happened after I came to know Patty during our first afternoon on the sand. She was sensitive and intelligent, and what I thought to be shyness was only concern about what she might say. As the day went on, Patty's roommate slipped further and further from my consciousness and Patty began to dominate it.

I think in that first afternoon we talked about everything that seemed consequential to us at that point in our lives: family, school, career, fears, joys, potentials, faith—all of the things that people are normally hesitant to express. And the conversation came so easily. My turning point was beginning to take shape.

The question was, did I want to commit myself to falling in love with a girl that was quickly becoming a good friend? That was not how I pictured the love relationship. I thought it was supposed to be more chemical, more vibrant, more volatile. This was warm. That's the best word that describes it: *warm*. I was concerned about that.

What is astounding is that I believe I have "fallen in love" with Patty over the years. I will say honestly that when I married her I don't think I was prepared to understand the magnitude that our relationship would take on in time. Perhaps no one really understands the special dimensions and special oneness of love. At this point, what I thought was going to be a "fun-and-games summer," in which I would often fall in love, changed into a summer in which I would learn to love one special person.

But summer does end; and when it did, I was forced to return to Harvard while Patty journeyed back home to Tucson and the University of Arizona. With her immediacy gone, the question was whether to take this girl seriously or drift back into the fun and games to which only college seniors are privy. During this period I was also being torn in opposite career directions. On one hand, my parents were tremendously proud of the fact that their son was attending Harvard, being enriched by scholars and scholarship. On the other hand, my own personal needs to express my musical talents were becoming stronger and stronger. It was Patty who was the most supportive about being a creative talent; and, interestingly enough, over the years that has not changed. There have been many times when I have been prepared to quit, but Patty has kept me trying.

It could be said, then, that I was a young man troubled by indecision, a young man at a major turning point. I had not only begun to allow music to dominate more and more of my life, I had also fallen into the nightlife syndrome of the club performer— good times with women and flowing liquor. While Patty was loving me in Arizona, I was loving anyone I could connive or con into my Harvard dormitory. It was late on one of these nights that my telephone rang while I had someone in my room. The young lady, thinking she was helping me, answered it; and Patty, on the other end, was crushed by the sound of another young woman. After my initial disgust with what I had caused to happen to someone I loved as much as I loved Patty, I faced the issue of what to do about it. You see, I had an out. I could end my relationship with Patty and go on with my bachelor's life or I could attempt to do something to win her back. The decision was obviously one I have never regretted.

I realized that none of us is autonomous; none of us really lives his life alone; and all of us need someone to mirror who we are—to bounce off the best and the worst of who we are and how we relate to others. I knew I needed Patty. Here was the recognition of a turning point. Again, I am mentioning it because it would have been just as easy for me not to have taken this moment seriously, not to have made a positive decision. Most of us do not gamble with our lives. We take the road of least resistance and lowest risk. That is not, in most cases, the way to go. I mentioned earlier that none of us sees himself as others see him, and that was the other thing I realized about Patty. If my own specialness was ever going to come through to be something valuable, it needed to be understood totally by someone else. That is something Patty and I have worked very hard at—understanding our own and each other's uniqueness.

When I finally made Patty realize how much I loved her, it was she who supported my pursuit of music—if that was what I honestly wanted to do. And it has been Patty who has climbed to the peaks with me and helped lift me out of the valleys. In colloquial terms, this turning point could be called, "know a good thing when you've got it and hang on to it." In my next turning point, the issue of hanging on became even more personal and far more serious. It was a moment of life and death—not my own—but the struggle of a little girl whom I love more than anything in the world.

My daughter Blythe is nine years old now and

loves everything that a nine-year-old girl should love, from dolls and gymnastics to school and Magic Mountain. It seems that there are no limits to her interests or her horizons. But there was a day, actually just minutes, frozen in my brain, held there—held like a recording—a time capsule that seems to play over and over and over again, forcing me to recount the most frightening moments of my life.

A Turning Point in Faith

We had just moved to California. Patty was out shopping and young Tommy was taking a nap. Our rented home sat high up in the canyons above Beverly Hills and, like so many homes in southern California, had a pool in the backyard. Because both of our children were babies at the time, I remember making a point of the fact that if there was a pool, it must be gated off from the rest of the house, and so it was. For us, just having spent three years in the cold country of New England, it was a wonderful luxury.

Blythe was constantly asking Patty or me to take her down for a swimming lesson, and now I wish she had had swimming lessons prior to our arrival in California.

The sun was beating down, making it one of those lazy summer days that lulls a person into going with the flow, not fighting the feeling and not paying quite enough attention, maybe losing track of someone he loves. I believe that's what I did—not pay attention. We'd been swimming for about fifteen minutes when the telephone rang. There was an extension next to our gated pool, and I picked Blythe up and sat her down next to me as I answered. It was my first major record offer, the reason for coming to southern California—the reason Patty and I had sacrificed our home on Cape Cod and treked across the country with our two children.

I remember that when I answered the phone, I was holding Blythe by the hand; but somewhere in the conversation, somewhere in my own enthusiasm, somewhere in the lazy haze of the California sun, I dropped her hand. As I hung up the phone, I heard a quiet splash, not really a splash, a sort of moving of the water. I was frozen, and all I could do was call her name. The first time I called, it was as if I expected her to answer. "Blythe?" Just a casual question.

Then with more anxiety, "Blythe?" Then with panic, "Blythe!"

Somehow, my body moved. Somehow it got me to the edge of the pool and into the water. I thrashed the water searching and searching for the child, this entity created by God and Patty and I. This "you-me person" as we used to call her. This child that we loved more than life. Finally, like an animal who realizes it's about to die and rolls over on its back with its paws up in the air, I stood perfectly still. For the first time in my adult life, I asked God to help me.

My prayer that day was simple, "I will pay any

price, give up anything, change anything if You'll just give me the grace to find my little girl." A simple prayer, a desperate prayer of hope, and then there was a sound. A sound that most of you wouldn't hear, not because you couldn't, but because you wouldn't. It was the sound of her air bubbles blipping to the surface of the water, blipping Blythe back to me. I followed the bubbles which led me underwater to touch her tiny feet; and grasping her body, I can remember leaping out of the water with some super-human power, a power that I have not been able to understand since that day. I expelled the water from her lungs and desperately tried to breathe life back into my child.

Well, she did breathe. And the sound was sweeter than any musical note I'll ever hear. She not only began to breathe again, but has continued to grow into her own special person.

Prior to this experience, I had been what I would view as a negligent father. Maybe because of my blindness, I chose not to participate as directly with the children as I could have. Realistically, however, I believe I chose that course because my interests were elsewhere. I could not relate to the early visuals of a baby's first smile, moving of hands and feet, the first facial expression of relationship between child and mother or child and father.

All of this was an excuse to cover up my own selfishness. I was struggling so hard for success, career, and personal gratification, that the children and even Patty were really just adjuncts to my life. This is not to say that they were unimportant, but constants that I took for granted. This confrontation with near tragedy has made me appreciate every moment that I share with every member of the family.

It's interesting that both this and my next turning point deal with life and death struggles. But sometimes it takes a hammer hitting us over the head to make us begin to realistically understand the significance of each life-experience. Life is a state of continuous evolvement. And the experience with Blythe on that summer day evolved my life to a place of utter humility and utter respect and caring for the lives with which we are privileged to be intertwined.

A New Look at Life
Over the next few years, the waves seemed to calm and life seemed to be flowing very smoothly. My career was moving up steadily. My children were growing up healthy. My marriage was becoming more and more defined. In general, I felt pretty good about myself, like a man sitting on top of a mountain looking down, feeling just a little bit sorry for everyone else who isn't quite as fortunate. How miniscule we are in the scheme of things! How quickly fate can deal a new hand.

One morning about three years ago I was taking

my normal run through the streets of the neighborhood and was approaching a hill where two or three
streets come together. As in any intersection, there
was a signpost with the names of the streets. It was
protruding slightly, and as I ran by, my forehead
caught the sharp edge, causing it to break the skin. I
probably should have had a few stitches, but counting
on the fact that nature would take its course, I let
it go.

After about five months, I noticed that the wound
was not healing correctly, never forming a healthy
scar; and I decided to go to a dermatologist for
advice. He examined my forehead and told me that I
had a very common-to-California skin growth. Upon
taking a biopsy, we learned that it was malignant, a
carcinoma, but certainly nothing to be alarmed about,
and he treated it with office procedures. After this,
we were to follow up with frequent check-ups, during
which time the doctor found and removed smaller
bits of the cancer on two occasions.

It was then decided that, due to the fact that I
was a public person doing frequent television shows
as well as movies and other public appearances, I
should have a skin graft done for cosmetic purposes.
That seemed reasonable; so while I was in his office,
he made an appointment with one of his colleagues to
do just that. When I saw the renowned head of plastic
surgery at UCLA several weeks later, he didn't waste
any time. His experienced eye diagnosed a cancer

that had been continuing to grow for three years. He wanted me in the hospital the next day. I didn't question his authority. There was something in his voice that made me nervous, something that said, "This is more serious than either one of us may realize."

After four hours of surgery, Dr. Miller told us that the tumor had spread beneath the surface tissue so the previous testing had not indicated the depth of the tumor. It was three days later when our phone rang with the unpleasant news that the pathology was not clear.

Dr. Miller said, "Tom, we are going to have to go in there again, but this time I would like some tests. I would like you to take the tomogram series."

"What's that?" I asked.

The tomogram is a series of head x rays that will indicate if there is any cancer on the skull. Not only were we talking about the possibility of losing the nerves that would allow my forehead to move with expression, we were talking about the possibility of bone cancer and the potential need for radiation or chemotherapy treatments.

Patty and I were stunned with disbelief. We were in a state of shock. Cancers of this kind are very, very difficult to arrest. All I could think of was that my time on earth might be much more limited than I had ever anticipated. My time to become all the things that I wanted to be—to become special—

might be cut off, bearing witness to our own human vulnerability. So here I was, a person believing that I had everything well in hand and zap, fate shuffled the deck.

The next morning, Tim Miller operated again, and again we were forced to wait through those days of eternity for the pathology results. As in each of the other turning points in my life, this one, too, had its potential for positive motivation. It was in my decision to appreciate every event relating to every day of my life—a hamburger, if it tasted good, became as important as a board of directors' meeting. My run on the beach every morning counted as much as a hit record. Hugging my children became more important than holding onto a dollar.

Thanks to Tim's surgical skill, the test results came out clear. My forehead was clean of the cancer that nearly took away the joys of my tomorrows. I can't begin to describe the relief and, in retrospect, I can't begin to describe the impact that an experience like that can have on a person's life.

It was following my battle with cancer that I wrote this chapter. All of us must come to terms with the fact that we face critical turning points within our lives. The question of what we choose to do with those turning points allows us to have positive control over our own destinies.

I think it becomes necessary here to try to define what I mean by turning points. A turning point is a moment, or set of circumstances, that holds within it long-term effects on the process of becoming all we want to be. Everyone's turning points are different. Not all of us relate to the same ones, although there are some we have in common—birth, death, marriage, medical crises, career choices. What is different for each of us is the particular set of circumstances that govern our recognition of our own turning points. Learning to recognize those circumstances and understand which ones are serious is one of the most important dimensions in human evolvement. There is no way that I can rub a crystal ball and come up with a methodology for each one of us in the process of search. The best I can do is suggest the premise that turning points can be recognized, and they are substantive to personal evolvement.

Turning points allow us to run risks, to become like Columbus—explorers of our own destiny—not necessarily reaching for stars, but for our own specialness. I truly believe that men and women living their own lives, seeking their own potentials, attempting to govern their own destinies live not only more fulfilled, but simply happier existences. Recognize your own turning points. Trust your own instincts. Roll the dice, spin the wheel, play the cards—go for it. The alternative is far more destructive.

Stumbling Blocks

Anger, fear, envy, and excessive competitive drive are, I believe, the principal stumbling blocks in our lives. Collectively, they are the major conditioning forces in our lives. All of us deal with these four elements; how we react to them, making them work for us positively or allowing them to affect us negatively, indicates how effectively we are dealing with them.

Fear

The first emotion facing all of us is fear. From the time we are born, we are forced to deal with things that seem alien to us and, consequently, cause us to be afraid. In my own case, my blindness caused a

The author relaxing beside the ocean.

myriad of confused and intense emotions. Just putting one foot effectively in front of the other without being frightened about what I might bump into was an immense undertaking. As a youngster, I was being conditioned by physical pain; and that pain translated into an abundance of fear, creating a certain withdrawal from life. It was not until the need for socialization and interaction became dominant in my life that I was willing to take a chance and not just walk, but run.

I began overcoming my stumbling block of fear on the school playground. I had been sitting, just squeezing a rubber ball, one of those wonderful ones that rings when it bounces and is large enough to be chased and caught effectively by a blind person. I loved the feel of the ball as I squeezed it tightly and then relaxed my hand, allowing it to fill my loosened fist. At one point, however, I squeezed it too hard and it popped loose and began to bounce its way across the surface of the playground. I was so upset by the loss of my ball that I forgot about being blind, forgot about the conditioning of pain. I jumped up and began to chase after the sound of the bouncing ball. Within about fifteen feet, I caught up with the ball, accidentally kicked it with my foot, and was forced to chase it again. The thing kept bouncing and bouncing, always away from me, and I kept wanting it more and more. Finally, I was able to come to a kind of bumbling, gripping stop with the ball clutched to my stomach. At that moment, I experienced a feeling of tremendous accomplishment.

That brings us to the formula which allows us to overcome our fears. There is nothing more exhilarating than the accomplishment, the triumph, of beating back our fears. The feeling of high excitement when we win even a small battle over fear is unrivaled and can come as a result of a multitude of small triumphs at any age. Think, for example, of the child preparing to attend summer camp for the first time. How many parents have forced their child into the backseat of the family car and driven into the mountains, facing a moment of tears and tantrums when they dropped their child at Camp Waupanata, or some such camp with an incongruous Indian name. They return in two weeks only to find that the child has turned his fear into tremendous accomplishment. He is even hesitant to come home again. He has triumphed over his fear of the unknown.

What If I Fail?

It is essential to come to terms with fear, to understand and deal with its ultimate human concern—failure. Whether we are afraid emotionally, that is, attempting to deal with some trauma that besets us, or whether we are physically frightened by the possibility of pain, we are really saying, "What if I fail? What if I cannot succeed? I am afraid to be a failure!" If that is the case, and if fear is one of the principal stumbling blocks confronting all of us, then overcoming our fear is based on our ability to measure the consequences of failure.

The Consequences of "No"

So often, the fear of failure is based on the consequences of someone saying "no" to us; thus, we say "no" to life before anyone else has a chance to say it to us. The most often exaggerated, ultimately confusing, totally ridiculous word in the vocabulary of mankind is *no*. We must learn to measure the effects on us of the word. *No* can span the spectrum from "not now" to "never." In whatever framework it falls, the word *no* is never, should never, must never be totally destructive to the essential framework of who we are in the evolvement of our own uniqueness.

The Japanese have solved this problem. They have a word which is used as we use *no*, but actually means "maybe"; and that is how I see the consequences of *no*—as "maybe." I am convinced that there is no such thing as an absolute "no"; there is only a stopgap in time. I cannot always convince other parties to believe as I do; I am sure, however, that even if I have to give up my immediate goal, I will find another way to be personally satisfied. The establishment of a balance regarding the word *no* will allow us to cope with what we actually fear, which is personal failure. With an accurate frame of reference, fear, then, can actually become a stimulus, forcing us to participate in a life activity and allowing us to push our anxiety aside, not making it a critical turning point. I pushed aside the conditioning of pain, the years of saying "no" to independence when my desire for that bouncing ball became greater than my fear of failure. In the final analysis, what Franklin Roosevelt said is absolutely true: "The only thing we have to fear is fear itself."

Envy

Just as debilitating to one's life as fear is envy. Attitude-revealing cliches—"The grass is always greener on the other side of the fence"; "We want to move uptown"; ". . . keeping up with the Joneses"—evidence the envy which surrounds all of our lives. Like fear, the degree of that envy indicates whether it will work to our advantage or disadvantage in the evolution of our lives. For the most part, envy is a stumbling block, something that stands in the way of our getting down to the business of living full and active lives.

Comparison

Comparison is such an odious thing. When I was a boy, I was constantly comparing my life, as I "viewed" it through blindness, with the lives of those lucky kids who could play football or baseball easily because they were able to see. I was so preoccupied with others, that I lost the most valuable thing any of us possess, and that is time. I certainly was not developing a positive self-image—something that none of us can ever do without. I particularly envied the guys who could play high-school football. To me, they were the epitome of successful young men. I wanted desperately to be a halfback, pounding into the line on Saturday afternoons and getting the date with the most attractive cheerleader on Saturday night.

Envy by Young and Old

Perhaps the most notable example of envy and how it functions as a stumbling block, especially in teenagers, is in the way girls tend to see other girls their age. How often did the tall, gangly, gawky kind of teenager envy the boy-chasing flirt, only to find out in later years that the qualities, those physical qualities envied in a flirtatious young girl, did her no good at all in formulating her life. Very often, that tall, gawky young girl turned into a beautiful young woman who succeeded in almost everything she did.

Envy is not confined to the young, however, for there are many men living their lives envious of the jobs held by other men. If the man who feels this kind of emotion could turn the envy into a motivating factor, which would push him to exert that energy in improving himself as a human being, he would probably surpass the person he envies.

Envy is a relative thing. What we envy today we

can hope, because of our evolution, not to envy tomorrow. That's a wonderful thing to consider. We are capable of putting aside the stumbling block of envy and replacing it with a positive sense of appreciation for the qualities in other human beings whom we admire. It is possible to turn a negative stumbling block into a positive feeling. Today, I would not want to change places with any of the young men I envied in high school. I have been able to grow as a human being and turn my blindness to advantage. The only people I now envy are those who seem to make better use of their time than I do and those who seem to be able to convey the emotion of loving one another with more directness of communication than I happen to possess. That is healthy envy.

Excessive Competitive Drive

The next stumbling block is one that took years for me to understand—the stumbling block of competitive drive. In my life, the need for competition was an outgrowth of anger; competition provided a way to strike out at the world in order to attain a sense of human equality. In my young mind, it seemed as though competition was all I could do in order to create a framework of human understanding between myself and my peers. The problem was that I carried it far beyond any sense of reason. I was obnoxious, arrogant, and, sometimes, even rude. It was necessary for me to be the best at everything, regardless of the cost to myself and anyone else with whom I came into contact. I made a spectacle of my accomplishments and even developed temporary feelings of hatred toward the person with whom I competed.

This excessive competitive drive carried through all parts of my life—from the classroom, to the athletic field, to music, and even into relationships with neighbors and family. I simply did not understand that the drive to compete can be as harmful as it can be positive; it can be as much of a stumbling block as an asset. It can turn off relationships and turn on anxiety.

In another chapter, we speak of turning points as major parts of who and what we all become. I faced a clear-cut turning point concerning the competitive drive which had become my stumbling block. I was a junior in high school and was beginning to achieve some national recognition through my wrestling. After losing my first six matches, I won the next couple of hundred in a row; and coaches and athletes around the country were beginning to believe I might have substantial talent.

The Consequences

I was competing in a dual meet with a high school team which was in our league, but was nowhere near our level of competitive proficiency. The boy I was wrestling had no business competing with me. From the start, I dominated the match. The only thing that kept my opponent in it, kept him from being pinned, that is, his shoulders forced to the mat, was the peculiar way he had of wriggling and squirming on one side enough to continue the match. By the third round, or period, the score was something like fifteen to one in my favor, and it was obvious that I would win the match with ease.

So, why not ease up just a little on my opponent? Why put him through an unnecessary beating? And that is what wrestling is, by the way, a physical beating. My own need to compete, to be recognized as the best, coupled with anger, forced me to drive my body again and again into his, to apply every technique I had learned through hours of studious coaching in order to punish my opponent into eventual submission.

There is a hold in wrestling commonly referred to as the guillotine. The name is effectively chosen. The premise of the hold is, basically, to use one's arms and legs to spread the opponent's as widely as possible. The opponent is then rocked onto his forehead and stretched. There is no attempt in this move to end the match, to pin the opponent. It is strictly a punishment. The hold is used more often in close matches when one person is lucky enough to assume a position he can hold throughout the completion of the period, a round. In my case, in this match, the move was uncalled for.

I applied my painful torture and stretched. Then I heard a horrible sound—the cracking of my opponent's collarbone. I was too good at my job. His scream of pain is something I shall never forget. Even though the young man whom I injured so badly may never realize it, his injury, the pain I inflicted on him, changed my life. At that time, my kind of competitiveness contained no element of appreciation for the talents of others and, in reality, was a tremendous stumbling block in my relationships with other human beings. This type of competitiveness resulted in nothing positive on my behalf. Thank God, from that day on, I was able to understand the limits of competition and to understand the secret formula of the competitor—that the reason for competitiveness is within the competitor. Others are only mirrors, measuring one's accomplishments. They should reflect an example of the excellence one can attain, prompting a competitor to stretch his abilities in order to obtain his own uniqueness. I do not condemn the competitive spirit, but as with any other quality in life, balance is required. The competitor is his own competition.

The Undercurrent of Anger

There is no question that the undercurrent of my competitive stumbling block was anger. I guess it is the undercurrent of my early life. Anger has been the dominant emotion in my life. It has been both the most positive and most negative effector of who and what I have become. It has carried me to heights and plummeted me to lows, as I believe it does all of us. As with fear, the primary reason for anger is fear of failure. We become consumed either because we are dissatisfied with who we are, or because we believe we are failing. In order to cover our weaknesses, to support our sagging egos, we strike out at others, trying to make excuses for our lack of participation, for not interacting effectively in society. I spent too much of my early life feeling sorry for myself and blaming my blindness. Because of anger, I gave up tremendous opportunities to succeed and to become mainstreamed into the flow of life.

Anger Must Be Directed

Anger must be directed constructively. It must be directed away from internal frustrations and turned toward principled, intelligent, external goals. When I lived my life competing, believing it necessary for me to be the best in everything I undertook, I was not focusing my anger toward anything which might be regarded as permanent. A temporary victory only prompted me to search for the next competition. When we learn to like ourselves, to become all we want to be and celebrate our own uniqueness, we can convert anger from a state of anxiety and frustration to a feeling of personal growth and social betterment. For example, every motivation I had in life through my growing years was to convert my blindness into something that did not exist. I seemed to continually be trying to force people into saying, "He's blind, but it doesn't matter. He's successful. He's a good boy." When I understood that blindness was one of the most positive forces I had in my life, I converted my internal anger and allowed it to flow externally, utilizing it for the betterment of my own and other's lifestyles. When anger becomes totally subjective, that is, personal, it loses the potential for objective application. Anger must be directed. It cannot flail around in our heads and then explode in random fireballs of anxiety.

Anger Can Be an Advantage

Today, I am just as angry as I was when I was a little boy, fighting against my inconvenience. The difference is that now my anger is directed toward the correction of the situation rather than the expression of a frustration. I have converted my anger from a disadvantage to an advantage. I have turned a stumbling block into a positive assertion of human strength. The loneliness of my fenced-in backyard and the alienation of competition have been replaced by the joy of human interaction through the open expression of appreciation for others, of love both for them and for myself.

So then, fear, envy, anger and excessive competitive drive are what I believe to be the four stumbling blocks governing many of our lives. They all, however, expand into a larger picture, the picture of human conditioning.

Conditioning

If you are beginning to believe that you are special and that "specialness" applies to everyone around you, if you are convinced that being "special" is the only way in which you wish to be evaluated by other human beings, then the question is, why have most of us not achieved the celebration of our own uniqueness, become all we want to be, and asserted our own individuality? The answer lies in our unwillingness to break away from a conditioned sense of who we are in the niche we have accepted for ourselves within the human social system. We are clearly unwilling to take chances, run risks, or lose little battles in order to win big wars. We vacillate, or rather drown, in public opinion and accept the superiority of others. We are individual human islands drifting in an ocean of ambivalent indifference.

Specialness, Confidently Asserted

We do not become valuable to others unless we are able to confidently assert our own specialness. This does not mean that each of us must become a world leader. It does mean, however, that we must look for those qualities that set us apart from others. We must assert those talents and enlighten others to those personal attributes, thereby accepting the opportunity to make substantive contributions to society and to the lives of those around us.

The stumbling blocks that stop one from believing he is special are the results of conditioning. This conditioning shapes a person in two basic areas: what a person thinks of others, that is, how he perceives them and their effect on him; and what he thinks of himself and how well he understands his own originality.

Reverse Conditioning

I am testimony to the possibility of reversing one's conditioning. I have carried with me all my life the stigma of blindness, the social label that has so often set me apart from the things I wanted to do and the people I wanted to care for and to share with. Though much of this separation was a result of how others viewed me, there is no question that most of the emptiness and loneliness I experienced were brought on by my own "fear-failure syndrome." When my belief in myself beat back the fears, I was able to take my active and rightful place in society.

There Are No Formulas

There is no formula that will open the magic door to the assertion of one's own uniqueness. There are only suggestions. Some may work for one person and some may not. The truth is that "not to try, is not to live."

The conditioning process falls into two general categories: negative and positive. It is the negative conditioning, however, that is often misunderstood. I believe that there are two forms of negative conditioning. These are negative-satisfactory conditioning and negative-dissatisfactory conditioning.

Negative Satisfaction

To be negatively satisfied may seem like a paradox, but it is not. The person who is negatively satisfied carries out his life in a pattern of passive acceptance. He thinks that, though "things could be better," it is easier to accept his life as is rather than face the possibility of anxiety or even disappointment. Most of these people are those of great potential yet moderate achievement. They are never self-starters and never leaders, even though they may possess certain of the necessary qualities of leadership. They deny themselves advancement or promotion in their work, believing that it is easier "not to make waves" or accept responsibility. Within their marriages, they are frequently angry and spend a great deal of their time complaining about what's wrong with everything around them.

Such a person is satisfied with the way life is, but in his heart he believes he could have been, and should have been, the president if he had really wanted to be. The person who agrees to accept his negative-satisfactory conditioning believes that the choices he has made are his own; but he also believes he could have changed his life if he had not been held back by environment, family, education, or any other excuse he can manufacture to hide his own disgust and support his sagging ego.

Negative Conditioning

Of the two kinds of negative conditioning, negative conditioning by satisfied acceptance is certainly the more difficult to change. The person who has accepted his place in life, though he thinks of himself negatively, is not angry; therefore, this emotion cannot be used positively for his improvement. This person never blames himself for his situation. His sense of reality is "if my environment caused me to be the kind of person I am and put me in my predicament, I am not responsible. So I will accept my situation and go on with my day-to-day, boring existence."

I think it is important that people who believe this way understand how uniquely special they really are. Each one of us does fill a niche in the human order of things. How we fill that niche will determine whether or not we achieve a semblance of personal balance and how well we project ourselves to those we love, aiding them in the development of their own self-images. In the evolution of life, there is clearly a symbiosis between all of us. Every contact we have with another human being on a day-to-day basis affects our evolvement and others' specialness. I can't emphasize enough, especially to those people who are conditioned to negative satisfaction, how much they mean in the upward evolution of mankind. All of us are not destined to be leaders, but we are all meant to make substantive contributions.

Leaders Are Negatively Dissatisfied

The person who is negatively dissatisfied finds his negative dissatisfaction on all social stratas, on every level of social evolution. He can be anyone from the poorest of the poor to a world leader suffering with that which he believes he cannot change. A leader in business, industry, education, science, politics, or any area that requires constant change and upward development lives within this framework of conditioning by dissatisfaction. Such an individual is angry, and the way in which he applies his anger will determine in what direction he will evolve. If his anger is applied destructively, he will tear down the foundations of his own specialness. He will be destroyed by all the stumbling blocks in his path. He will be considered too aggressive, too radical, too cocky, and, eventually, at those moments of his turning points, he will be torn down by his own ineptness; and rather than function from a position of confidence, he will freeze under stress. Positive application of his anger, however, can make him become all the things he believes he can be. He will have recognized his negative conditioning, turned it around, and made it work to his best advantage.

Redirected Anger

The best example of redirected anger is found in the rise of the consciousness and standard of living of minority groups here in America. The negative conditioning of the minority was the public view of the group. A dissatisfied attitude about that conditioning prompted members of the minority to apply themselves and excel. As they expanded, loved, and created new lives, their children benefitted from the other part of the conditioning process—positive reinforcement by parents who had turned around the negatives and created environments that recognized the basic premise of this book, the belief that each person is special.

Developing positive conditioning will force an evolvement of a positive self-image, and self-image is the most important part of success. What others think of us counts a great deal, but what we think of ourselves cannot possibly be overestimated.

Egotism Is Necessary

Right now it probably sounds as though I am selling large doses of egotism. And that is absolutely true! The question of how a person projects himself is what really counts. The question of how he projects that self-image will determine whether others see him as a self-effacing idiot or as a confident person going about the process of self-actualizing his life. There is nothing more annoying than the pompous egotist, yet there is nothing more comforting than competent confidence.

Consider, for example, a situation in which all of us occasionally find ourselves when we are most vulnerable. A person has decided that something is seriously physically wrong with him and goes to a doctor, a healer, a person who can put him right again. It has been my experience that most doctors are capable and confident people; however, occasionally, we all have met a doctor who, because of his own insecurities, is not sure of himself. He makes a quick diagnosis without the correct application of tests. He is abrasive and short with his patient and gives the impression that the illness isn't worth his time. His supreme over-estimation of his under-developed talent makes the patient totally uncomfortable, besides endangering his health.

On the other hand, in every person I have known who has, through positive conditioning, developed an effective self-image, one absolute is present. That quality is humility—humility prompted by the understanding that though he may know a great deal, he is humbled by that which he does not know. What enlightenment this can be for all of us.

Conditioning Can Be Changed

I should note here that none of our conditioned qualities are absolute and unchangeable. I am an example of someone who made the negative-conditioning transfer based on the fortunate evolution of knowledge. I could just as easily have been negatively satisfied as negatively dissatisfied. My anger from dissatisfaction had to be redirected toward a positive attitude. Our greatest human moment is when we take negative conditioning and turn it around to our advantage, and this can never occur without positive interaction with others. Once turned around, we open the world and our lives to a panorama of possibility.

Each Person Is in Control of His Life

Each person must evaluate himself, his wants, needs, and talents. No one can do it for him. The process, however, is not immediate nor without setbacks. To stumble is not to fall. To trip on the road to successful evolution and the discovery that you are special is not to lie down and accept the status quo. The only stumbling block that cannot be overcome is death, and even that can be delayed in some cases by utilizing effective self-image. We have not yet begun to tap our will to live or our courage and our desires. I am not advocating some form of unreality; I am only suggesting the utilization of what is possible. Becoming aware of who we are in relationship to our conditioning will allow us to come to terms with ourselves. We will never find our own specialness until we find a balance between what is possible and what we are conditioned to be. If we can accept a margin of failure, understanding that none of us achieves all the things he wants to, we will be willing to try a little harder, protecting ourselves against what we must admit would be inevitable disappointments. But in trying a little harder, in that search for possibility, we will be wondrously surprised at our own accomplishments.

Personal Satisfaction

There is no greater sense of personal happiness or personal satisfaction than at those times when we are amazed at our own achievements. Conditioning is the perception of ourselves as we struggle in life against our own stumbling blocks, and the most subtle obstacle of all is the human measuring process. We are constantly comparing ourselves, as others are constantly comparing us, to our peers, and these comparisons may stimulate us to over-achieve or force us into believing that we are not as good as the people surrounding us. Again, we need balance and self-perception; reflecting and marveling at the accomplishments of others is not in and of itself harmful, but comparison is. None of us knows the struggle of another well enough to make an accurate analogy.

Conditioning by Parents

How many times has the progress of sons and daughters been either delayed or destroyed by parental pressures for and expectations of equal success. How many times do we hear, "His father was a doctor; his grandfather was a doctor; so he must be a doctor," even though he may want to be a guitar player in a rock and roll band. Conversely, we often hear, "Her mother and grandmother were satisfied to stay home and take care of the children, so why should she want a career and not even be interested in marriage?" We are finding ourselves coming to grips with a system of labels again, this time seen through our own conditioning.

Delays Are Inevitable

Stumbling blocks are inevitable. Conditioning happens to all of us. Delays in reaching goals can be guaranteed. But so can the achievement of your potential, the evolvement of uniqueness, and the awareness that you are special.

Special People

All people are uniquely special and each of us finds his own uniqueness on an individual level. The stories which follow are not about extraordinary people. In each case, the specialness is a result of the personal triumph of an ordinary person over adversity. In each situation my perception of the adversity was that it was far greater than it seemed to them. For each, the decision to participate in life by overcoming personal obstacles was a day-to-day function of individual personality and courage. I am not attempting to downplay the battles that my friends have won. I believe, however, that we must come to terms with the fact that, whereas the hurdles of others may seem insurmountable to us, for them,

Tom and Dinah out for a morning stroll.

those difficulties settle into a daily routine of struggle and then conquest.

You may read the succeeding stories and say, "If I were in that situation, I couldn't do that." But you would be incredibly surprised to find out that my friends would probably find whatever situation in which you are involved extremely difficult for them. Each of us has the same decision to make—to fall into the pits of depression and despair or take a firm stand and deal with our situation day by day. If there is one thing each of these people has taught me, it is that out of despair can come a better soul, a better spirit. Out of the drama of life's struggle can come the ability to turn adversity into positive reinforcement of our self-image. Every negative can be turned into a positive. Right now, you might be saying, "That's easy for you to say, you've found a way to make it; but our problems are not the same." For me, or for anyone, blindness is a traumatic struggle, and I feel I have taken the positives in my life and made them work. But the people I am going to introduce you to now have coped with adversity far greater than my blindness.

My friends vary in their inconveniences, but each has overcome something that the world labels a "handicap." From epilepsy to cancer, from blindness to shortness, my friends have learned about their own uniquenesses and have begun to live their lives based on the premise that they really are special, sometimes because of their inconveniences, never in spite of them. My friends also vary in age from a senior citizen to children too young, too innocent, too adaptable to even realize that they, too, have incredibly performed a miracle in adjusting to life in this world. All my friends, however, have this in common: They love life, they love others, and they love themselves because they know that they are special.

Patty Wilson

My first friend was forced to realize her potential very early in life. Her name is Patty Wilson and she is now eighteen years old, beginning her freshman year at Brigham Young University. She loves music, history, boys, dancing, and just about every kind of sport there is. Patty's family is extremely athletic with the exception of Dotty, her mother. Dotty is a nurse who spends most of her time taking care of the constant injuries that her family of athletes sustain from time to time on their way to individual accomplishments and glory.

Patty told me that very early on she was aware that her coordination didn't seem to be as good as the other kids', especially her brother's and sister's. She was always the *klutz*, tripping over something, losing her balance, never quite achieving a "poetry in motion." From speaking with her mom and dad, I have determined that they were not aware at the time that Patty might have a more substantial problem, a problem that would cripple almost anyone else.

Patty's first awareness of her inconvenience came when she was in the third grade. One day in the classroom, her body suddenly began to convulse. Convulsion is the loss of control over motor reflexes in the body, and with that loss goes the ability to control the attitudes of others toward the afflicted person. What a horrible wrenching of human identity: Patty was instantly a freak, instantly different, instantly dependent! She was only nine years old then; and when she asked her parents to explain what was happening to her, they could give her no answers. They did not know what caused the convulsions which left her in a catatonic state, and more upsetting was the fact that the doctors to which they subsequently took Patty had no explanations either. The entire family was frustrated. They had no place to turn, no knowledge to draw upon, no cure to hope for. For the next four years, the seizures continued without anyone being able to offer assistance of any kind. Through that period Patty had to face the humiliation of peer group ridicule and the fear of not knowing when or where she might suffer another seizure.

An old axiom states that love is the best medicine

for most illnesses, and the Wilson home had love in abundance. Patty was given tremendous support from all the members of her family, who have provided the constant nourishment necessary for her ego and sense of self to survive. Her positive self-image, in turn, has fostered the belief that people could, should, and would love her.

When Patty was about twelve years old, she became interested in the fact that her dad ran every morning. Along with millions of others, Jim was caught up in the American jog-a-thon, as all ages, all shapes, and all sizes took to the roads of this country morning, noon, and night, hoping to rekindle the flame of physical fitness. One morning Patty asked if she could go along. In the beginning, she ran less than two hundred yards. The human body and spirit, however, is the most unbelievable of all creations; its potential for expansion and improvement is endless. Patty's two hundred yards quickly became two miles and then five miles every day with her dad. During this time, Patty's run would sometimes be interrupted by the seizures which no doctor could explain. She suffered the constant embarrassment of their occurrences at unpredictable times and places. Her father was a continual source of calm strength. He kept Patty from hurting herself, while encouraging her to run.

Although her parents were outwardly calm, they were anguishing over their inability to help their special child. They were being shattered by the thought that something was wrong with their daughter and they could not understand what it was. Patty's distance had grown to ten miles by the time the doctors determined that she was a "grand mal seizure" epileptic. "Grand mal" is the most complex of the three forms of epilepsy and the type most people picture when they think of an epileptic. During a grand mal seizure the epileptic totally loses control and can even swallow his tongue. It is shocking and terrifying to anyone who has to deal with it.

Even after learning of the exact cause of the seizures, Jim and Patty kept right on running. One day they decided to run to Patty's grandmother's house, about thirty miles away. They surprised her, arriving in time for a hearty breakfast. Because of her running, Patty's confidence was growing. Even though the seizures continued, she began to believe that she could live a normal life. Though she had epilepsy, there were still activities in which she could become involved, pursuits that could fill her life.

What was possible with her running? Patty had already decided she would not win any trophies for speed, so running short races—one-hundred yard, four-forty, eight-eighty, or the mile—didn't seem to make a lot of sense to her, nor did the twenty-six miles of the marathon. But what about longer distances?

At fourteen years of age she and her father set out on a run from Alameda to San Diego, approximately two hundred and fifty miles, running an average of thirty to thirty-five miles a day—longer than any marathon. This was not to be the only distance goal that father and daughter would accomplish; it was only the first of many.

They made another run from their home in Orange County to Denver, Colorado—fourteen hundred miles. That is two hours by jet, two days by automobile, and over forty days of pain and agony on foot. I, myself, run eight to ten miles a day. There are some days during training when the pain is such that I believe my legs could fall off; and that is running under the best of conditions—along the ocean where the air is clear, the roads are good, and there are no hills, much less mountains. I asked Patty why she made a run of this kind. Her answer was one given by many a famous explorer, athlete, or adventurer: "Because it was there. Because I trained for it."

What happened to Patty on that 1400-mile run has to be something unlike anything that has happened to most people in the pursuit of conquering adversity. Four days into her Denver run, she felt something crack in her foot. She completed the day's running and went back to the trailer which her mother drove, always waiting for Patty and her dad to arrive. By the time Patty arrived at the trailer, she couldn't even get her shoe off. Her shoe had to be cut off. And when her father looked at her foot, he froze, because he was aware of the kind of pain she must have been going through. You see, Patty Wilson had broken two of her metatarsals, the bones in her foot.

Her parents rushed Patty to the hospital where x rays were taken. When the doctor explained what had happened, he suggested the obvious. "Put a cast on it and stay off of it for at least six weeks." Patty explained what she was doing and asked if she could go on. The doctor said in amazement, "How could you possibly consider going on? If you try running on that foot, you may never walk on it again, let alone run." Jim has told me about the tears that the entire family shed. The feelings of loss, of being crushed, of failing after months and months of preparation. Yet it would not be failure for Patty Wilson. She was determined that no matter what the doctor said, she was going to run.

I admit that I question the logic that allowed her to continue to run on a broken foot. I'm not sure that in that position I could allow my child to subject herself to that pain, but the Wilson's did. I am convinced that they did so out of total love for Patty, not for the glory, not for the press, not for the ego gratification, but simply because they clearly understood that this run was critically important to Patty.

For over forty days, twelve hundred more miles, Patty Wilson ran on a broken foot. Stop, if you will, and consider what most of us believe to be painful. We can go to bed with a common cold. We stop everything we're doing for a headache; and if we have the flu, we might as well be dying. Picture all of those pains and amplify them to begin to comprehend the pain Patty felt each time her foot hit the ground. I cannot conceive of anyone with more courage than that.

You would think that making that kind of effort would be enough, but it was not. As soon as her foot healed, Patty began training once again. This time she was preparing for the longest run ever made by any woman—three thousand miles, from Seattle, Washington, to Washington, D.C. To me, that kind of mileage is incomprehensible.

Something had changed for Patty now. She was becoming aware of her own uniqueness and her ability to participate in the lives of others who suffered the same inconvenience. She became involved with the National Epilepsy Foundation, an organization started in 1970 to raise the American consciousness about epilepsy and to help epileptics understand the possibilities that still lay open to them. Patty realized that the foundation was in serious need of funding and she decided to make her three-thousand mile run worthwhile, not only financially for that foundation but for every other human being who shares the misunderstanding and abuse that comes with the label of epilepsy.

She and her family, especially her father, became an army looking for ways in which they might raise money through the process of her run. They contacted corporations, running clubs, church groups, anyone who might participate and be willing to pay a little money to share some part of Patty's experience. To date, this seventeen-year-old girl has raised over $300,000 for the National Epilepsy Foundation. By the way, she did finish that run—three thousand miles and a few more in ninety-four days— from Seattle, Washington, to the Capitol Building in Washington, D.C. Her feet trod over five million one hundred thousand steps. Doesn't it seem possible for each one of us to start with just one step? One step that initiates our desire to be more than we are; one step that takes us closer to finding our own uniqueness; one step that makes us understand that we are special.

Though epilepsy is the oldest of man's maladies, we know very little about it. It is a subtle disease. In fact, unless a person is told that a certain individual is an epileptic, I doubt that he would realize it. Only in the cases of seizure would he be confronted by it. Though the shock is traumatic, an epileptic can go through most of his daily life without obvious confusion. It was once believed that the gods used epilepsy to set apart from the rest of mankind those whom they favored. Julius Caesar used it to create the mystique surrounding the greatest of all Roman Emperors. The point is, epilepsy was always viewed as something that made the person who had it different.

The underlying framework of Patty Wilson's

story is that difference is terrific! Difference can be beautiful! Difference, well-applied, can provide the impetus for becoming more than a person would have become otherwise. The "difference" works to one's advantage. It can reinforce the uniqueness that one is struggling to attain. Remember the days when athletics of any kind for women was frowned upon and discouraged? Or remember the bookworm who was chastised by the rest of the class? How often have all of us been labeled or put in a category which stifled and limited our sense of who we are and what we could become!

Patty Wilson chose to take her label and make it work to benefit not only herself and those she loves, but multitudes of others who suffer from the same inconvenience. She is now planning one more run. This time she will cross the continent from New York to Los Angeles, and she has asked me to put my true grit on the line and join her. This is a challenge that I have yet to accept. Perhaps I have sown enough daredevil oats for a while; but I know this, she can count on me to be among the fans supporting her on the sidelines for any future run she attempts. I am so proud to know her, to be inspired by her, and to love her. She has profoundly changed my life and I hope that reading about her might profoundly change yours.

Rice Brothers

The next story I would like to share is about two new friends of mine who have a label that cannot possibly be avoided, one that clearly sets them apart from others wherever they are. They have used their difference and its label to their own best advantage. Gregg and John Rice are twins who stand three feet, two inches—all of it dynamite!

The world in which Gregg and John Rice must live involves great adjustment and compromise. Their story is not one of remarkable "little" men. It is a story of unique courage, absolute human purpose, definition, and most importantly, of love shared between two brothers and the belief that two people, each three feet two inches tall, equal one person at

*Tom and Patty often head for the golf course
to enjoy one of their favorite sports.*

six feet four inches with two heads and two absolutely remarkable brains. My friends have never, at any point in their lives, felt sorry for themselves. On many occasions they may have felt frustrated and angry, but self-pity has never accomplished anything for anyone and has certainly not been a part of the lives of Gregg and John Rice.

A Positive Self-Image Is Hard Work

The positive self-image they now have did not come easily. It developed over many years through dealing with rejection and self-doubt. John and Gregg are smaller than most five-year-old children, weighing about fifty pounds. That is less than my seven-year-old son, Tom. Try, if you will, to picture being unable to reach the doorknob to open the door and enter a room, or having to stand on a stool which you had to drag over from somewhere else in the house in order to brush your teeth. Think of being too small to reach the blackboard during school days. Think of the constant frustration of dealing with these "little things" each day. I met John and Gregg after seeing them on a segment of a television show, and one of my first questions to them seemed, as I look back now, typically stupid and insensitive. I asked, "Where did you guys grow up?"

"Grow up?" they asked. "We never really did that, but we were raised in West Palm Beach, Florida, famous for its palm trees and millionaires."

A Successful Role-Model

To compound their problems, Gregg and John were abandoned by their natural parents. But they were raised in a foster home by people who came to love them dearly. Though Palm Beach was Florida's playground, John and Gregg's family were, at best, lower-middle class. As John said, "We were raised on the other side of the track." Their father was hardworking and a good provider, but the men feel they never really had a male role-model to follow. This does not mean that John and Gregg did not love their parents and were not loved in return. It only means that in their particular situation, there was no one who prompted them to believe that they could be successful—until the evangelist came to town. Following is an excerpt from a speech given by Gregg Rice in Detroit:

I can remember, even as a boy, going to the revival meetings and having my mother set us in the front row, watching the preacher arrive in a big black Cadillac, wearing those multicolored suits with the carnation in the buttonhole. I thought, "If I ever want to be a success, I'm going to have to learn how to be quick with words," because that's all he seemed to do. When the offering plates would come back, heaped up and running over, I'd say, "That looks all right to me," except that neither John nor I got the calling for the ministry.

Success Comes After Work

I soon discovered that the only difference between the people that lived in Palm Beach and our family was simply in the way they thought. I realized that the only place where the word "success" comes before the word "work" is in the dictionary. I feel tremendously lucky to have come to understand early that everyone needs a goal, and I guess my first goal was to have my own car.

At seventeen I got involved in a direct sales cosmetic company. Avon didn't look bad to me; and I thought, "Why couldn't I do the same thing?" Anyway, I went down to the Chevy dealership and got pictures of a red Camaro. I put those pictures all over my wall and looked at them everyday and decided that that was what I wanted.

After three months in the business, I was able to buy that Camaro; and it wasn't long afterwards that my brother John bought a duplicate.

Identity Crisis

Early in their teenage years, John and Gregg lost their foster parents and were forced to confront an already difficult identity crisis alone. In Gregg's words:

Our dad died when we were in the eighth grade and our mother, two years later. She was a pretty bright lady, though, and she demanded from our brother that he get us into college. She was aware that we would probably not be able to do physical labor, and she was sure that the only thing we could hope for in our lives was to develop our minds.

The counselor who was assigned to us said, "Look, there is no way you are going to easily find people who will hire you because of insurance reasons." If I hadn't developed a positive sense of myself at that time, I might have packed my suitcases and headed home. But we stuck it out. We stayed for one year, sort of in the front door and out the back. I'm glad our mother didn't say how long we had to be there.

We completed that first year but decided that it was going to be necessary for us to get out into the everyday world and make a living. Somewhere inside of us there was a drive for success, and it couldn't wait for us to finish four years of school. After working within the cosmetics industry, as sales-trainers for a few years, we decided that, with the construction boom going on in south Florida, real estate was the place for us. I don't want to underestimate the work we had to do. I guess maybe none of us see ourselves as others see us, and I'm probably not telling you about the drama involved in trying to learn to adjust to society. I mean, obviously, things like dating and school activities and developing real friendships have come hard for us. Somehow, through sticking together and caring about one another, we've found a way to get by. Anyway, we did choose the real estate business, and in our first year we sold fifty-seven homes. I guess I'd better say that we closed fifty-seven homes to this point in the year.

Important Possession

The college that we attended has since asked us to come back and give a motivational seminar. On that occasion we pulled up in our big red Cadillac. . . . The first guy that came out to meet us was the same counselor who believed we would fail. He had a big grin on his face and said, "You know, Gregg, I always knew you guys were going to make it." And I said to myself, "Why didn't you tell us that then?" I wonder how many people have sat across the desk from that guy and had him tell them that they couldn't make it, robbing them of their most important possession—their dreams.

Humor Is Always Needed

I'm convinced that the most important quality that a person has in this life is a sense of
humor; and in the real estate business, we've
had a lot to laugh about. Imagine what it is like
to come into a house with a prospective client
and have the owner's child think that a playmate
has arrived! Last week I was in a home and I
heard noises behind me. When I turned around,
this cute little three-year-old had brought out all
of her toys and was inviting me to sit on the floor
and play with her. I thought, "In twenty years
that house might be worth two hundred thousand and she might be a prospective customer."
So I sat down on the floor and played with her.
You know, by the time I excused myself, my
customer wanted to buy the house. I guess that's
really taking advantage, but good guys can finish first.

We've driven people crazy writing ads for
our listings. My broker said, "I can't possibly
put this ad in the paper the way you've got it
written."

"Why not 'lovely knee-deep shag carpet'?
It's just about knee-deep to me?"

"But breathtaking baseboards?" he asked.

I'm the neighborhood baseboard expert. One

time we were called to speak to a group of roofers in Florida, and I said it didn't make any sense for them to be calling us; we are only carpet and baseboard experts! So you see, we've learned to have fun.

From the Shoulders to the Sky

I guess that is the most important thing I can tell you. You have to learn to take who you are and make the most of it. You know, I've even had people tell me I'm lucky to be three feet two inches tall, because the success I'm having is due to the fact that I am small. Let me tell you how lucky I am. Doorbells are too high; elevator buttons are too high. Hey, if that's luck, who needs it? The harder I work, the luckier I get. The secret to success is that it doesn't take much of a person to become successful, it just takes all of him. A person isn't measured from his toes to his head; a person is measured from his shoulders to the sky. I believe that there isn't a family in America in which the mother and father can say to their kids they don't have a chance to succeed. I believe that we live in a country in which success is possible to each of us, if we are willing to take every opportunity that presents itself and make the most of it. That's what John and I have done. I'm sure that's what is possible for each and every one of us. I think that a man or a woman can even reach the stars if he or she is just willing to stand on tiptoes a little bit. One thing we have proven is that life's battles don't always go to the biggest, strongest man, but to the one who tries. In the end, the person who wins is simply the person who thinks he can.

Be Yourself, But Be Motivated

Gregg and John exemplify the truth that as long as a man is willing to try, he can assert his own specialness. He can celebrate his own uniqueness. He can become all the things he wants to be. The story of John and Gregg Rice is unique. It could even be said that their story relates to the positive input of people who have learned to recognize that their difference could be turned into advantage. But the issue they confronted, the assertion of their uniqueness, is no different from anyone else. We all face the question of being motivated, and we all face the simple truth of having to look at ourselves in our own lifestyle mirror and decide if we are making the most of who and what we are.

As an afterthought, I asked John and Gregg if they had ever considered what they might have been if they were six feet tall. Both of them laughed at me and responded exactly as I expected them to. "Well, we're not sure what we might have been, but whatever it was, we wouldn't have been as good at it as we are at being ourselves now."

Contentment Can Be Found

Every special person I have ever known has been a person able to find contentment when viewing his own achievements. That does not mean contentment from quitting or retiring or stopping the process of growth. It does mean, however, contentment in the kind of person he has become and will continue to grow to be. A special person is one who *recognizes* who he is, what obstacles he must overcome, and then, simply *does* something about it. People who excel, because of a unique talent, that is artists, musicians, or athletes, are wondrous to behold; and their accomplishments should not be de-emphasized. People who excel without an obvious talent, those who overcome a complex adversity without the aid of unique gifts, are far more interesting. Selling fourteen million dollars of real estate was not enough for the Rice brothers; they turned their interest to public speaking and encouraging others to success. They are absolutely remarkable men.

A New Horizon

These incredible men, who have so remarkably conquered the world of real estate, have now turned to one of the world's toughest businesses—show business. John and Gregg left Florida and their careers, moved to California, and filmed a pilot show for a new television series. In the series, they will portray landlords of a pair of zany detectives and maintain order in a world of mystery and murder.

Even in make-believe, John and Gregg Rice continue to keep a proper perspective on life.

In the years to come, it will be interesting to see just how far these men, inconvenienced by size but blessed with big hearts and creative minds, will go. For all of us, John and Gregg Rice provide an inspiration and an example of successful people who are truly measured from their shoulders to the sky.

Ann Gell

My next friend has had the unique opportunity of seeing life from two varied perspectives. I think her sense of relevance and her awareness of the joys of life might help all of us come to terms with the equality of human potential and possibility.

Ann Gell lives in Iowa and is now attending Oberlin College. I met Ann while I was giving a concert in Illinois. She and her mother came backstage after my concert, and I was delighted to meet a young woman who was poised, confident, seemed extremely sensitive, and obviously had a tremendous zest for life. It happened that Ann, too, was blind. We spoke of many things—the problems of being a teen-ager (Ann had just completed her sophomore year of

The author rehearsing at his piano.   141

high school), of her hopes and dreams, and of the obstacles she thought might be in the way of those dreams. She was one of those people to whom, upon meeting, one feels tremendously close, as if one had known her all his life. Before they left we agreed to correspond by cassette during the following year.

A Miracle

Well, Annie was wonderful at keeping in touch with me; but at the end of a six-month period, when I had failed to keep my part of the bargain, her tapes naturally stopped coming. I wasn't overly concerned. I knew that she was busy at school and I with my work. Three months later I received a cassette that I will never forget as long as I live. Ann's voice was shaking, trembling with an enthusiasm unlike any I had ever heard before.

She said, "Tom, you're not going to believe what's happened. I guess that I don't believe what's happened. Tom, I can see again!"

I sat frozen. Annie could see! I should explain "see again." Up until the time she was three years old, she had had sight. Now through a brand-new surgical technique, about fifty percent of the sight in one eye had been restored. So I sat there, listening to her as she described all the things that were emerging from this regained, but also newfound, sense. I realized that Annie now had a perspective unlike anyone else's. Not only could she see with her eyes but, from her years of blindness, her other senses had also become well-tuned. Those benefits, coupled with an absolute conviction that life is terrific, resulted in an astoundingly positive and happy young woman.

The first thing Ann saw when the bandages were removed was her doctor's face. She told him he was ugly! I don't know if he believed her or not; but I'm sure, at that moment as far as Annie was concerned, he was the most beautiful thing in the world. That sight was followed by one of her family. What a wonderful sight that was! She'd lived for seventeen years knowing her family, but all at once that limited knowledge was expanded.

A Problem of Perspective

At first, the most difficult task for Annie was a perspective on dimension. What she had only touched, she could now see; but she had no depth perception. Consequently, she found that she could not at first fully understand the possibilities of her new gift. Annie told me she had to look at something and then try to compare it to what she knew it to be, based on her other sensory knowledge.

Three days after her surgery, Annie looked at her first magazine. In it was a picture of a well-known and well-publicized Hollywoood beauty. She asked her mother a remarkable question. "Mom, is this girl beautiful?"

"Well, everyone says she is," her mother responded.

"Gee, I guess I don't know what beautiful looks like."

Her mother tried to comprehend what her daughter had just said. "I guess beauty is in the eyes of the beholder, Annie."

"I guess it is, Mom. I guess I'm going to have to learn about what is beautiful."

"No, Annie," her mother said. "Just appreciate everything that is around you."

And that's what Annie has done. Her favorite flower is not a rose; it's a dandelion. She is "hung up" on her dog's tail. Best of all, Annie has no sense of prejudice or hostile judgment based on visuals.

True Focuses

I had the opportunity of sharing Annie's first trip to New York. I thought her story was so incredible and was so touched by it that I wanted to introduce her over television to the entire nation. The night before the show was taped, we planned to have dinner at a restaurant. When I came to pick up Annie at her hotel room, the door was slightly opened. I politely tapped on it, but I guess she didn't hear me. I stood in the doorway and heard her crying.

"Annie, what's the matter?"

"Oh, nothing, Tom. I've just been standing here looking at the lights of the city and I can't believe it. I can't believe that so much light is generated from an invention of man."

That's what Annie has done for me—generate light, putting back into focus my own sense of myself. She helped me remember that I am so lucky. I have the God-given right to experience daily joys that can be unrivaled if I choose to make them so. Annie reconfirmed my belief that everyone is special, everyone is unique. I hope her story can do that for you, too. I hope you will remember and think about the fact that you, too, are special.

Annie's favorite thing to look at is a rainbow. Within the rainbow are all the colors of the prism, and I'm sure Annie appreciates each one of those colors, just as we must learn to appreciate each nuance of life. We must come to understand that the negatives are only temporary stops along the way to a positive reinforcement of our own specialness. We must learn that there is so much to know. When we understand how little we do know in the overall scheme of things, then we can realize how much we are allowed to grow and experience all of life.

Art Lucas

My next friend is a man who faces death each day. In spite of this, or perhaps because of it, he is able to daily celebrate life and his own special place in it.

I met Art Lucas at a party and was impressed with his vitality and enthusiasm. Although Art told me he was sixty years old, I knew I was talking to a man not only younger in spirit than myself, but obviously in better physical condition.

About a week after the party, I took my guide dog and went for a walk on the beach. I heard the sound of someone's feet coming up behind me. Soon, a friendly voice called, "Hi, Tom. How are you doing?" as the man ran by. Forty-five minutes later, I

Tom, with his guide dog, jogging
near his home.   147

heard footsteps approaching me and then that same happy-sounding voice said, "Beautiful day, isn't it, Tom?" I found myself turning around as quickly as I could to jog along with the owner of that pleasant voice.

The runner was Art Lucas, just over sixty years old; but after almost an hour's running, he still found it possible to communicate with me as though he hadn't been exercising at all. Within about four minutes, however, my lungs were rasping; and I found it difficult to breathe, let alone carry on a conversation. I kept thinking, "This man is sixty years old; you're twenty-eight. What is going on here?'

The Beginning of Friendship

At the end of my half-mile, Art asked if I would like to start running with him in the mornings. I grudgingly accepted his offer, feeling sheepish about my lack of physical fitness and ability. Over the next three months, I developed a love-hate relationship with Art Lucas.

Every morning, precisely at 7:00, the phone would ring and that same cheery voice would be urging me out of bed, not only to get up but to be prepared to run. The beach was waiting. Most often, my response was less than virtuous and I hung up the phone, wondering why I had ever gotten myself into this trap of daily running. No more than ten minutes later, Art's horn would be beeping for me.

Running is something that doesn't come easily but requires hard work and diligence. Lucas never let up on me, and I think one of his happiest days was when youth prevailed and I was able to run further and faster than he. It was also on that day that he began to tell me something about himself.

I had decided that Art was some crazy runner who only ran for physical fitness and my company. I discovered Art had other reasons for running.

Throughout his life Art was always willing to take a chance to compete for the golden ring, to try the long risk for the great score. He had a successful business career, had lucratively invested in the stock market, and had been willing to try everything from bamboo farming in the swamps of southern Louisiana, to investing in cemetery plots. All in all, Art has always been a man of courage and vision who, in most cases, had been a consistent and exceptional winner. But at the age of fifty-seven, his life took a different turn.

A Race Against Death

At that time, Art was plagued with a constant and annoying sore throat. At the insistence of his wife, Betty, he went to a doctor who told him it was probably only some kind of allergy and prescribed an antibiotic for the condition. After three months, however, the condition had not been alleviated and

Art decided to go to UCLA and see a different doctor. The doctor noticed a problem he diagnosed as lymphnode cancer, a third-degree melanoma. After further tests he informed Art that there were surgical techniques that might extend his life, but the chances for long-term survival were minimal. In fact, the doctor gave Art three to six months to live.

Art underwent extensive surgery involving the removal of the lymph nodes which resulted in loss of most movement in his right shoulder. Surgeons removed half his tongue; and his mandible, or lower jaw, was so badly broken that speech and eating were virtually impossible. For the next three months, Art could only eat through a straw, and his senses of taste and smell were completely crippled.

Love of Life

After this debilitating ordeal, most people would have given up and set about only to wait for death. Art Lucas, however, loved life. He loved his work, his family, his existence. He believed in his own uniqueness, and he was determined to assert his own specialness. As soon as he was able, Art began a physical fitness program.

He first took a rock that fit comfortably in his hand and began a few simple squeezing exercises to rebuild some of the destroyed muscle tissue. He started walking just a half a mile a day. That walk turned into a mile, then two miles; then Art began jogging. The exercise paid off as Art rebuilt his physical strength enough to withstand two more surgeries.

When I met Art, it had been a year and a half since his last operation; and my description of the man running along that beach that day certainly indicates that he fooled the doctors and was not about to die. His perspective, his appreciation for life, is unbelievable. While running one day, Art said to me:

Tom, when I was thirty years old, I could have been physically fit and mentally alive. I could have run, but I chose not to. I'm sixty-two years old now and I am feeling better than I ever have in my whole life. Why should I feel that I'm growing old? Why should I feel that my productivity has stopped?

Considering that it has been nine years since Art's ordeal began, it can be safely said that Art's cancer is in remission and that his prognosis is as good as any man's his age—probably better. Art believes that his experience has made him a far more sensitive human being; it has enriched his life, it provided a belief in himself. Art now knows that he can make contributions to society that he never before believed possible.

Rewards

Although Art left the large corporation for which he worked as an executive, he is now running four smaller companies of his own and makes more money than he had previously. More importantly, he feels better about himself than ever before.

Throughout Art's business career, he tended to be a father who placated his children rather than participated in life with them. He felt that his dialogue and communication in general had lacked humanity. He had put his family into a fixed space and not allowed them to enter his world.

A Zest for Life

His family has changed in the last nine years; they all are much closer. Art is now a grandfather adored by all his grandchildren, and he enjoys each minute spent with them. His relationship with his wife, Betsey, has grown into a mutual participation in things they both love. Today, Art Lucas is stretching to touch the limits of his own specialness. He believes in his own uniqueness and his own good fortune. He is making the most of who he is and loving every minute.

For myself, I have never had a friend who gave me more of a true perspective on life. Art rechanneled me and put me on a track of well-being. My limited words can't thank him enough, for I have learned that he who is about to lose his life can sometimes find it more readily than he who takes life for granted.

Special Children

There are some very special, special people in this world: and those are the children. Children who have a terminal illness or who have come into this world "inconvenienced" are special by the nature of being alive; yet they are blemished due to genetics or a creative force who knew far more than we what a human being can tolerate or what values these children can teach us (or learn themselves) despite their inconveniences. Those are the special people I would introduce now—children who have made an incredible contribution both to those human beings with whom they have come in contact and to the field of special education. The courage of my next group of friends far outstrips that of any other I have been

Tom resting a moment from the
morning run.

privileged to witness.

Specialness Should Be Appreciated

If I have learned one lesson in life, it is to appreciate and relish specialness, whenever or wherever I find it. I cannot say, "Oh, isn't that terrific. What an emotional story." I have learned to appreciate that essence of courage, which I believe is commitment, and try to incorporate it in my own life.

Due to the legislative passage of bills 503 and 504, handicapped children can no longer be discriminated against in their claim to a public school education. This law is a magnificent step forward in the history of our country; however, passing a law and making it work are two totally different battles. Part of the law deals with the interaction of handicapped children, and, in this area, the battle has just begun. For instance, a muscular-dystrophic child has a great physical problem eating lunch in a public school cafeteria, not to mention the emotional difficulty of coping with the stares and ridicule of the other children.

Though children are most innocent, they are also most honest; and that honesty can, unfortunately, at times be cruel. Nothing can be more damaging to a handicapped child than those honest evaluations from normal children. The child with multiple sclerosis may have a very gifted mind but because of speech-motor difficulty may not be able to express in simple words what he or she feels. His own frustration is magnified by children mimicking his speech. A blind child who cannot learn the geography of the school building finds himself lost trying to find a classroom, bangs into open doors and is eliminated from active participation in athletic programs designed for normal children.

There are also other types of "inconveniences." An albino child may go through life relatively normal, except for the fact that his or her pigmentation separates him, making him completely different in the eyes of other children. Whatever handicapped suit a child must wear, the stigma is still the same: *different, alien, dependent.*

The legislature can pass laws that hypothetically allow the child to participate as an equal, but it cannot pass laws that govern the social stigma placed on that child by his peers.

Special Children

I first met these special, special children during a conference for the President's Committee on Arts for the Handicapped, held in Washington, D.C. I had been asked to participate in the closing ceremonies paying tribute to those young people from all parts of the country who were involved in school programs developing their artistic skills.

During these ceremonies, I witnessed everything from interpretive dancing by the deaf, to wheelchair basketball, to a lovely quadriplegic girl who paints by guiding a brush with her mouth. These were all very special accomplishments, but I was not prepared for what I saw next.

The People Behind the Play

About five hundred people were crowded into one of the rooms at the Kennedy Center, sitting on the floor and witnessing the performance of a play. This was not just any play, but one called *Special Class*, written by Brian Crawl and funded by the school system of the city of Las Vegas. *Special Class* deals with the interaction of handicapped children within a public school. The play was written with one goal in mind: to develop for the handicapped child a vehicle that allows him to express his feelings about what it is like to participate in a special class within the public school environment.

The play deals brutally with what is and is not possible for inconvenienced children; but it celebrates the potential of each one of those children and emphasizes the specific choices which each can make: either to live passively, allowing the handicaps to close him in, or to rise up and participate in love and happiness each day.

The particular handicaps of the children in that play were different in kind and severity: from blindness to juvenile arthritis and multiple sclerosis in combination with spinal, muscular atrophy. After viewing that performance in Washington, I felt compelled to find out more about these very special children and the special adults who wrote and produced the play.

A Dynamic Director

Every time someone reaches out and makes a major contribution to humanity, there must be a central driving force. In the case of *Special Class*, the driving force, the energy, the dynamic consistency that makes it all happen, comes from its director, Jody Johnson. It is impossible for me to find the words to describe the energy of this lady. She demands excellence from her children—not just the handicapped children, but the two hundred or so more that participate in her theater group called the Children's Rainbow Theatre. Her overriding goal is to mainstream these normal children with the handicapped children for the betterment of both. Some of her handicapped children have been allowed to make the transition from the play *Special Class* to other productions of the Rainbow Theatre. Most recently in *Oliver*, Steven, a twelve-year old with muscular dystrophy, played one of the orphan children; and Robin, fourteen, with multiple sclerosis and juvenile arthritis played the town drunk.

Jody's mother was comedienne Totie Fields. Jody watched her mother die from a fatal illness that never broke the spirit that prompted Totie Fields to participate with others. I believe it was her mother's positive example in adversity that led Jody to help handicapped children evolve into special people who choose to live each day as fully as possible. Jody expressed her philosophy this way: "Just because an instrument has a different shape, doesn't mean it can't play a beautiful tune." How magnificent!

Special Children Are People, Too

Although I wanted very much to understand the children who participated in this remarkable stage production, I found myself hesitant and a bit frightened to meet these children on a one-to-one basis. Here I was, a blind adult, constantly referred to as one who has overcome his inconvenience of blindness, yet I found myself feeling uncomfortable when exposed to these very special children. This feeling taught me something, too. It is not easy to become participants in their lives until we recognize their unique specialness.

It was easy to "watch" *Special Class* from a distance, to observe it as a wonderful tribute to the courage of handicapped children; but when I had to pick up Wanda and Steven, twins who suffer from complex-dystrophic disease, hold them in my arms, and feel their broken and open spines, I found myself cringing until they began to giggle and say, "I won't break! Hang on, Tom!" How much they taught me!

The children's interests span everything from

ham radio to the raising of Maltese puppies. Some have even entered their dogs in competition and won ribbons. As I met their parents, I found that most of them, too, were caught up in relishing each day's experience, not in the burdens of remorse and sadness. What noble profiles in courage they were; yet, given the alternative choices of depression, of feeling lost in a crisis, of giving up, why shouldn't they choose the road of hope and possibility?

Following my first exposure to *Special Class* at the Kennedy Center, I was determined to bring the play and the children to public attention. I was able to share the privilege of being with those special children of *Special Class* on Christmas morning in 1979 over American television. My memories of the filming of the story are surrounded by my feelings of personal good fortune; because of these children, I know that our tomorrows hold unlimited potential.

Having Fun

Although science has made wonderful progress in the elimination of childhood diseases, many of the children who participated in *Special Class* will not be here to reap the benefits of potential cures. That was my heavy burden while shooting the story, but we had some wonderful moments and many humorous moments. Picture, if you will, thirty handicapped children in all kinds of contraptions, along with six adults and a seeing-eye dog going into a Mexican restaurant and ordering the sloppiest, juiciest food imaginable and loving every minute of it. We certainly celebrated our own uniqueness!

In Celebration of Uniqueness

And in those wonderful, carefree moments, I forgot the questions hanging over so many of these children. I forgot, because they forgot. They were not thinking of how bad or how sad things were. They were only enjoying each moment of their experience. They were only asserting who they were. They were only trying to make the most of each moment they had. And that fact is what makes these special children really special. Specialness for them is not their inconveniences, but the fact that through courage and determination and, for the most part, the constant presence of pain, these children have miraculously achieved the realization of a unique life, a full life. They can forget the pain and the uncertainty, at least for a little while, and get on with the process of living.

Do not extend pity to my friends. They don't want it. None of us sees himself as others see him; and my friends, those particularly special children, don't see themselves as particularly special. They only see themselves as people who made the simplest but most important choice. That choice was to participate in life without backing off. The choice was to believe in their own uniqueness even if the form of that uniqueness might, to the world, be bent or distorted. Their choice was to assert that uniqueness, to celebrate it, and, through it, to evolve their own specialness. This is the choice that is also offered to each one of us and one that we can accept or reject.

A Crisis of Faith

Don't eat meat on Friday. Kissing with feeling is a mortal sin. People who do not believe in the Catholic Church will not go to heaven. Divorce and planned parenthood are not acceptable in the eyes of God. All of these thoughts, plus the fear that God would punish severely, made up my young, blind, Irish-Catholic faith. Religion was presented to me then with severe emphasis on sin and punishment. Restrictive commandment was given priority over values and virtues. And God was portrayed as a strict judge.

I lived my entire childhood in fear of sin and death. Coupling these fears with my anger about being blind, my distorted sense of faith made God too

Tom and Dinah—united in
necessity and love.

much for me to deal with. So, rather than deal with Him at all, I decided that God would have no real relevance for me. I journeyed through adolescence with no significant relationship of any kind with God.

As I asserted my individuality, I became, for all practical purposes, an agnostic; not atheistic, I didn't go so far as to say that there was not a higher power; I simply chose to believe that a relationship with God was only for those who needed Him as a crutch. I thought that to employ God as a part of evolvement toward success meant that time had to be taken away from the process of *doing* in order to ask. And to ask meant that I didn't believe in myself enough to grow into all the things I thought I ought to be.

What an absolutely egotistical and absurd frame of reference! None of us is immortal. None of us realizes his own specialness without the help of someone else; and that something or someone else is God. I am convinced that God gives us enough grace or strength to achieve our own specialness. That grace is the special power that allows us to make effective choices. I feel that He gives us the ability to assert our own specialness. Our grace is God's hope for us. We clearly are capable of making effective decisions which move us toward a oneness with Him.

Newfound Faith

This feeling of oneness with God did not come easily for me. It came when my daughter was drowning in our swimming pool and I felt absolutely helpless to do anything about it. I asked God for help, to somehow find my little girl. I was given that help. Employing my own human skills, employing the ability to hear her air bubbles on that June day, I was able not only to rescue her, but also to revive her. I am convinced that, though the power to hear her air bubbles came from the human mechanism of the ear, the impulse that made me listen to those bubbles came from another source.

In this book, I have constantly stressed the need to develop the potential that each and every one of us possesses. I am sure that God expects us to find His truths through the development of our individual persons, brought on by the day-to-day experiences that are unique to each individual.

I am not inferring that faith is a simple course, or that it has to be so much a part of our outward appearance that we overwhelm others by it. Faith can be quiet and subtle. I have met many Christians who have allowed the way in which they believe to negatively affect their lives. They allow what they think is "God's will" to turn them into ineffective pawns in the human game of life. The needs, selfishness, and cruelty of others pound them into ineffectual creatures who never assert themselves.

I owe so much to Patty for helping me find a realistic awareness and relationship with God. She is a consistent believer without making it overly obvious or uncomfortable for others. She quietly goes about the process of her journey to oneness with God someday. For a time, she had considered the possibility of dedicating her life to the sisterhood; but after a short stay in the convent, she came to believe that that life was not for her. I am convinced that she was meant for me. She has helped me grow to be a far better person than I thought possible, and much of that growth has come from her consistent example. For her the belief in God is closely connected to the responsibility of growth and of using all of the talents that God has given her. For her, self-actualization is finding that fulfillment, that peace, and that specialness in oneness with God.

Living Faith

There has never been a saint who was not a participant in interaction with others. I am so pleased to have come to a personal comprehension of my relationship with God. It has changed my life. I seem to have found a sense of inner peace and outward fulfillment. Along with Patty, this fulfillment was made possible through the example of two very special friends. I believe these two have truly come to understand the relationship between faith and the evolvement of their own individual talents and personalities. This knowledge has brought them to the celebration of their own uniqueness.

I was introduced to Tim and Carolyn Foran by

Tim's brother David, who has worked and traveled with me over the last few years. It was a mutual interest in the game of golf that opened the doors of friendship. Tim is one of the finest young teaching pros in the country. As I am always interested in any new techniques, suggestions, or equipment that could improve my game, it was only natural that the three of us spend ample time on the golf course to come to know one another quite well.

I was in an incredible slump, and Tim was trying to help me regain some semblance of the golf swing again. His quiet but assertive approach to golf was so refreshing to my shattered nerves, and his ability to articulate what he thought I should do was so unique, I began to believe that I might some day begin to play this game again. I learned that he had at one time entertained the possibility of playing on tour with the pros but had found that he was not prepared for the lifestyle. This discovery followed an Irish-Catholic upbringing much like my own, and a stint in Vietnam —two things which can distort one's self-esteem and self-awareness. Carolyn had grown up in a loving, close-knit family in New Jersey and had become a primary school teacher. I've never met two people who love each other more or who have worked harder to communicate with each other. It interests me that when I asked them if they felt they had always been happy together they agreed that for the most part they had been, but that their happiness had really just begun when they mutually asserted an essential part of their lives—faith. Had I had to face the crisis of faith that they did, I do not believe that I would have come to the kind of affirmation of God that they have.

Tim had become a golf pro at the only major country club within the city limits of Philadelphia. He was gaining a national reputation with his literary contributions to *Golf Digest* and other periodicals. His pro shop and lesson tee were both very active. He and Carolyn seemed to be living an idyllic life, and they very much wanted to have a family. Carolyn was soon with child and she enjoyed a normal, relatively comfortable pregnancy with no complications. But then the hand of fate dealt a new game. Carolyn gave birth to a Down's syndrome baby.

Crisis of Faith

Such an occurrence is extremely rare; Down's syndrome is usually associated with the pregnancies of older women. There was no reason to think that this could happen to them. The baby lived for only a few days, but in those days Tim and Carolyn experienced the anguish of knowing that although they had wanted so desperately to give life, healthy life, to their child, they had failed. To live through the pain of those days, knowing that the child they had given birth to could never take his rightful place in society, must have been pain beyond my ability to comprehend.

When the ordeal was over, and God had mercifully taken the child, Carolyn and Tim felt absolutely empty.

All the questions started. Was it Tim's fault or Carolyn's? Could they have done anything about it prior to giving birth? Guilt ran rampant. They went to doctor after doctor who found no reason to believe that either of them was responsible for the birth of the Down's syndrome child. "Then, why us?" they asked. And the answer kept coming back: "We don't know."

Seeds of Faith

For some reason which neither of them can explain, they began reading the Bible and sharing it together. After a time, they felt a sense of participation, something exciting and new in their relationship with God. And the seeds of faith began to take root. Along with those seeds began the feelings in both of them that they might once again try to give birth to a child.

There was no reason to believe that their first experience would be repeated. All the tests had proven that the possibilities of having another Down's syndrome child were one in a million. With their newborn faith and the assurances that this kind of tragedy could never be repeated, Carolyn again became pregnant.

At the beginning of the third trimester of what

had been a very joyous pregnancy, Tim and Carolyn, following their doctor's advice, decided to have the amniocentesis test to verify the health and normality of the fetus. Again, the doctor assured both of them that what they were going through was simply a formality and that everything was going to be all right. However, by some quirk of fate or cruelty of destiny, the test results came back indicating that Carolyn was carrying a second Down's syndrome baby.

A Living Miracle

My heart aches when I imagine the anger and total desperation they must have felt. Why did this happen to two people who loved each other so much and who were now establishing a belief in and love of God? I readily admit that, if I had been in their shoes, I don't know that I could have coped with all the feelings of frustration as courageously as they did, nor would I have come away with a greater faith in God. In my situation it might very well have been the reverse.

But Tim and Carolyn are so special; and at that place and time, rather than pulling away, they together moved toward God. They prayed hard and tried to understand the reasons. They tried to believe that God had a plan in all of this, that somewhere in His divine essence the assertion of who they were to be and who their children were to be must have had some divine intervention. The second baby, like the first, was not with Tim and Carolyn long; but unlike the first loss, the second was much more difficult to accept. And still, the roots of their faith somehow held firm. I am sure, in years to come, Tim and Carolyn will reflect not on the deaths of two children, but on the rebirth of two Christian souls.

It was about two years later when they decided to try one more time to have a child; and they made this decision with full knowledge and acceptance of the possibilities of having an abnormal child. If it lived, no matter what the circumstances, they would love and care for it. For the third time, Carolyn became pregnant. As the months went by, their anxiety, worries, and concerns grew. Yet their faith in a just God reinforced the roots of their belief in themselves and in His kindness. Every friend and relative was praying along with them, and for them, and for a healthy baby. Miraculously, they had come to a sense of peace that I guess I find difficult to understand; but God understood. In March of that year, Tim and Carolyn Foran were blessed with a full-term, healthy, beautiful, perfectly and wondrously normal baby girl. As I write this, Wesley is about eight months old.

Strength of Faith

Everyone who has the kind of faith that Tim and Carolyn have will have the same miracles. But their faith has not limited the assertion of their own individuality; it has only enhanced it. They are a marvelous family who have achieved an incredible oneness with God. I admire them and love them for their courage and envy them for their strength. I admire them for their Christian participation in life. I admire them for their ability to live their faith. To me, Carolyn and Tim exemplify the faith spoken about by the Psalmist in the following passages:

> The Lord is my light and my salvation: whom shall I fear? The Lord is the strength of my life; of whom shall I be afraid? . . . For in the time of trouble he shall hide me in his pavilion: in the secret of his tabernacle shall he hide me; he shall set me up upon a rock . . . . Blessed be the Lord, because he hath heard the voice of my supplications. The Lord is my strength and my shield; my heart trusted in him, and I am helped: therefore my heart greatly rejoiceth; and with my song will I praise him.
>
> Psalm 27: 1,5 and 28: 6,7

I believe that all of us must at some point turn to a faith of some kind. We simply do not stand alone. At some point we face those moments that simply outstrip our capacity to cope. It is in those moments that we must turn to a higher power, and that power desires us to expand our own specialness through the assertion of our own uniqueness, the celebration of that uniqueness, and the acceptance of a joyous *challenge* to develop that specialness.

Dependent
Independence

There is a social order to everything, an evolutionary spiral upward. When Darwin wrote of the evolutionary spiral, I don't know if even he realized how much he had said about the species. No matter what our hopes, inspirations, dreams or possibilities may be, they must find their fruition in interaction with others. I like to think of this frame of reference as dependent independence.

Because of my own struggle to find the specialness that sets me apart from others, competing against the constant handicap of blindness, I had good reason to understand the delicate balance of too much or too little dependence or independence. People who suffer from obvious physical handicaps seem to

The author tees off with his wife
spotting the golfball for him.   177

be the most blatant examples of those who either accept too much pity and dependence or are totally unwilling to accept any help at all, possessing an overabundance of independence. They spend their whole lives trying to find some midrange of acceptance. I think, within the focus of their struggle, they provide a striking example of the relationship between one's own specialness and that of others.

How often have we overestimated or underestimated each other and the relationships between us. Earlier I spoke of what it was like for me to live in the fenced-in yard built by my parents both to keep me in and other children out. When I was finally able to begin an interaction with sighted kids, I found myself clinging to every moment in which I thought I might be able to be with them. I remember sitting in my fenced-in yard in my swing waiting until 3:15 for their school down the road from my house to end. That meant that Billy and Mike Hannon, two boys who lived just next door, would come running up the street and open the gate to my yard, setting my life in motion with the enthusiasm of their friendship and play. When they didn't come on Saturdays and Sundays, often for good reasons such as dental appointments, too much homework, Little League practice, or any other legitimate excuse, I found myself crushed by the loss. This reaction of hurt is not confined to children. How often as adults have we held a job in our companies and then found that someone we felt was our friend was, at the same time, competing for our position? Was that person wrong? I don't think so. Friendship is earned over time and must stand the test of that time.

Specialness Comes from Within

The assertion of our own specialness cannot be dependent on the fulfillment of that specialness by others. It must come from ourselves. We must be our own catalyst. We must take the first steps toward celebrating our own uniqueness and becoming all that we want to be. Please don't consider that what I am saying is alien to the most important of all emotions that we all have, and that is love. But the correct application of love as it relates to our lives must directly connect to that other important word: share. And that implies emotional commitment of one human being to another. Each human being must be a separate whole, aware of and accepting his own specialness, in order to be able to love and to share.

There is no greater gift, no greater moment, than when we realize that we are loved. Those moments are rarer than the loveliest of precious stones and lovelier than any precious possession; and so they should be. We constantly overestimate and overuse the words and emotions that bind us intricately together. What we must learn to do is celebrate each other's uniqueness within the focus of how it affects and can aid us. On that basis we can appreciate excellence without envy. We can cope with disappointment because we are not crumbled by someone else's imposition on our lives. We can objectively utilize, as it were, the best input from everyone with whom we deal in the evolution of our lives. This attitude is neither selfish nor self-assertive; it is realistic. If we are to accept our own uniqueness, it becomes necessary to recognize the needs of others, and those needs are not our needs.

Enjoy Others

As a child, I structured an emotionally protective shield for myself that allowed me to be able to hold at arm's length all those who were not directly involved as significant participants in my life. That arm's length was not rude or cold or even distant; it was simply the evaluation of what impact people had on my life, and a correct filing system that enabled me to avoid the hurt of consistent disappointment. You can get on with the business of life if you learn the rules of dependent independence. How silly it is to waste a day hurt or angry at something or someone you cannot control. We must learn to evaluate whether that human being really counted in the long-term essence of who we are and what makes us special.

It is so much easier to be realistically sensitive when we realize that other people with whom we come in contact, with whom we interact in the day-to-day process of life can draw from us kindness, consideration, and compassion by the nature of sharing essential human qualities and taking up space on this planet.

It is not necessary to impose personal commitment on every inter-human relationship. For the moment, think of your own specialness as purely selfish. If you do, you will realize that interacting with others is the simplest way to evolve into all that you want to be. Learn from others, enjoy others, share what makes them unique. Evaluate their uniqueness and make it a part of who you are. There is nothing wrong with the hungering to be better, to be more, to grow. The entire purpose of this book is to prompt you to do just that, and you can do that best by learning from the uniqueness of others.

Necessary Balance

I'm suggesting a balance, a balance between dependence and independence. The discovery of this delicate balance, this tightrope of life, is not easy and takes constant trial and error. If, however, you have been evolving your own positive self-image, when you fall off the wire, you will land in a net built of personal experiences and the assertion of a belief in yourself. What a wonderful thing to say, "I believe in myself, uninhibited by the needless emotional strain of overestimated personal attachment."

The simple truth, the common denominator, is that anything that we become and all that we reach for must find its spaces first and foremost in the decision to be special. That decision must be made by utilizing, not abusing, dependence on others while, at the same time, clearly and totally asserting the independence of ourselves. We must begin now. Time is the one thing none of us has. Each of us must relish each moment, live each day, share each minute—for ourselves. And that assertion of self, applied with consideration, warmth, and caring, will make us far more valuable to others and, in that sense, far more personally enriched. The circle of giving does work. What you give eventually comes back. It is the price you pay while giving that is important. Learn to evaluate, learn to understand what you are willing to give and what you honestly have the right to expect from all with whom you come in contact.

Different Levels of Dependent Independence

There is no question that there are a number of variables in this formula. We each need different levels of dependent independence. Some of us by nature are leaders, and it is necessary for some of us to be followers. All of us, however, must answer the same relevant and relative question. Are we becoming all the things we want to be? Are we asserting the best that we have for ourselves, not for anyone else? And if, in the relationships that count, the special ones, the treasured ones, the unique ones, we are not giving of ourselves, how can we expect to gain anything from anyone else? I know that my words are direct and tough and may offend those people who may be saying, "What a selfish soul he is; how can he put forth this kind of premise after the wondrous life he has had?" What I am purporting is reality. What I am offering is the best of possibilities for each one of us. What I'm asking is for you to try to find your own balance, recognizing that there are ways to minimize personal human participation and actualize the joy of each and every moment that we are allowed to spend on this earth.

Become all that you want to be, knowing that it is totally up to you, but knowing, also, that your growth may stimulate others to grow and prosper. Dependent independence gives each of us a stake in the other. The assertion of specialness will find its modus of operation in the willingness of others to do the same thing. We are not alone, and I am sure that together we will succeed.

A Joyous Challenge

As you read these pages, I'm sure you were saying, "All right, where's the method? How do I convert these character studies and biographical sketches into a system that works for me?" How do I put this data into concrete terms that will help my growth?" Of course, if I had a foolproof method that would allow any given individual to assert the uniqueness that is within him or her, I would perhaps be doing more than writing this book. The truth is, there is no "method," no formula for the celebration of one's own uniqueness, only the possibility of participation in life.

You and I, all of us, are wondrously, magnificently, spontaneously alive. We know who we are.

The seashore provides a moment of relaxation for both man and dog.

We perceive our own essences and, with that rationale, separate ourselves from all other creatures. For any of us, that joyous awareness ought to be enough. Frankly, it *is* enough. It offers us the possibility of turning ourselves into even more than we thought possible, moving beyond our present own self-images, reaching higher than expected. We can truly be surprised. One starts with little goals which, when achieved, evolve into something uniquely exciting; and the wonder of all of this is that reaching our goals is clearly relative to who we are. It is not necessary for us to achieve according to someone else's standard of excellence. We *are* our own criteria.

The Danger of Comparison

It helps when we measure our accomplishments against those of others, but it is not necessary in the actual determination of how we are doing. Too many of us have felt the pain of failure when measuring our accomplishments against those of other people we have known. There is no variable as helpful or as damaging as the comparative shopping for human accomplishments. Think of how many times families have been irrevocably damaged when parents compared their children to each other, expecting one to measure up to his older brother or sister. Psychologist after psychologist has discussed this particular familial battleground when evaluating the human condition. Freudians to client-centered therapists unanimously agree that the damage done by these types of parental expectations is unrivaled in the complex textbook of human personality.

If I believe comparison is so odious to the development of the human spirit, why have I labored so hard to force you, the reader, to compare his life with those of people I have known? The answer is simple. My friends are shining examples of what is possible. They are not meant to make you feel less than you are. If anything, my goal is to make you feel far more alive, recognizing that you are much more gifted than you have ever let yourself believe and that you have not yet begun to tap your own natural human resources.

If we recognize, then, that life is a continuing process of evolution, we clearly become aware that none of us achieves his absolute goals. Goals are fleeting things. When we achieve a given plateau, we are only, as it were, resting, preparing for the next exciting climb higher up the mountain of our daily challenge. That daily challenge can and should be a challenge of joy.

Most of us are so programmed by negative conditioning that we never really enjoy the accomplishment of our own goals. We are hung up in failure and self-doubt rather than in exciting accomplishment. This is when we must assert a positive self-image. The term self-image has been so overused in the writings of psychologists, religious leaders, educators, and authors that I am hesitant to employ it. I have, however, come to understand that the development of a positive self-image is paramount to the evolvement of self-fulfillment and specialness.

The Assertion of Self-Image

Our greatest challenge, then, is the assertion of this self-image and its projection into each activity in which we are involved. I have already spoken of my own overdeveloped self-image that was carried to the point of alienating those around me. That framework is never healthy. The assertion of positive self-image allows us to accept limits, either imposed on us by our situations or by other human beings. We must spread our feet apart and develop a firm center of balance. We cannot be supermen, but neither are we passive acceptors beaten down by the dictums of others.

The German word *Mensch* describes the way in which I would like all of us to think of our own specialness. Loosely translated, *Mensch* means total person, and that total person is one who comes to terms with his self-image and its relationship with others. To do this, one needs to focus specifically on the events of the present, giving them total concentration. Since none of us is a fortune teller who can accurately project beyond the immediate, we must learn to accept who we are in our present condition. What has happened before is only relevant to how it affects what we will do tomorrow, and what we will things around today if you so choose. The decision to believe in your own value, which would seem to be the easiest decision that any of us could make, yet the most important, is probably also the most complex and the one that eludes us sometimes for a lifetime. Yet this quest for self-assertion is an exciting challenge. Utilizing every tool in your personal toolbox will plant the foundation of specialness deep in the soil of stability and potential.

This book represents one person's crying out with joy in trying to draw you into the unique possibility that each life possesses. Your own essence makes it possible; your own self-actualization makes it definite. You are special; no one can take it away from you. You are special; allow others to understand it. You are special; allow yourself to believe it. You are special; and I, along with every other human being, acknowledge that specialness. Projecting that specialness into every activity will change your life. Nurturing that specialness day by day will make for constant achievement. Without this day to day fertilization, you will dry up; and if that occurs, no one else will lift you up or feel long-lasting personal sorrow about your failure.

Each Makes His Own Choices

Though all of us are concerned with the well-being of others, in the end we must make our own choices. We must decide that our own uniqueness makes us worthwhile. That striving for the things we want, need, and love must principally come from us. Though people will reach out a helping hand of support, we face our own individual moments of truth alone. The adoption of a positive self-image will allow us to get through our turning points. The acceptance of faith will allow us to reflect on a higher power giving us the strength to understand that sometimes we can reach beyond ourselves and gain the help of someone far greater. Believing in the essential goodness of others will allow us to extend unlimited kindness which I am sure will be returned tenfold. Though the skeptics do not agree, life does work. God is in His heaven and, though all is not well with this world, we are still evolving, still growing, still moving in what would have to be an upward spiral of human accomplishment. We are participating in the most dangerous, but certainly the most exciting, part of human history. Mankind can do more now than ever before and can continue to do more in years to come. With the assertion of the specialness found in each one of us, we are all necessary. We all count. We all can make contributions. The decision is up to each one of us. Will you and I become all we can be? Will you and I celebrate our own uniqueness? Will you and I become special? Know that you can, for you *are* special.